Preparing Effective
Special Education Teachers

WHAT WORKS FOR SPECIAL-NEEDS LEARNERS

Karen R. Harris and Steve Graham
Editors

Strategy Instruction for Students with Learning Disabilities
Robert Reid and Torri Ortiz Lienemann

Teaching Mathematics to Middle School Students with Learning Difficulties
Marjorie Montague and Asha K. Jitendra, Editors

Teaching Word Recognition:
Effective Strategies for Students with Learning Difficulties
Rollanda E. O'Connor

Teaching Reading Comprehension to Students with Learning Difficulties
Janette K. Klingner, Sharon Vaughn, and Alison Boardman

Promoting Self-Determination in Students with Developmental Disabilities
*Michael L. Wehmeyer with Martin Agran, Carolyn Hughes,
James E. Martin, Dennis E. Mithaug, and Susan B. Palmer*

Instructional Practices for Students with Behavioral Disorders:
Strategies for Reading, Writing, and Math
J. Ron Nelson, Gregory J. Benner, and Paul Mooney

Working with Families of Young Children with Special Needs
R. A. McWilliam, Editor

Promoting Executive Function in the Classroom
Lynn Meltzer

Managing Challenging Behaviors in Schools:
Research-Based Strategies That Work
Kathleen Lynne Lane, Holly Mariah Menzies, Allison L. Bruhn, and Mary Crnobori

Explicit Instruction: Effective and Efficient Teaching
Anita L. Archer and Charles A. Hughes

Teacher's Guide to ADHD
Robert Reid and Joseph Johnson

Vocabulary Instruction for Struggling Students
Patricia F. Vadasy and J. Ron Nelson

Preparing Effective Special Education Teachers
Nancy Mamlin

Preparing Effective Special Education Teachers

Nancy Mamlin

THE GUILFORD PRESS
New York   London

© 2012 The Guilford Press
A Division of Guilford Publications, Inc.
72 Spring Street, New York, NY 10012
www.guilford.com

Printed in the United States of America

This book is printed on acid-free paper.

Last digit is print number: 9   8   7   6   5   4   3   2   1

Library of Congress Cataloging-in-Publication Data

Mamlin, Nancy.
  Preparing effective special education teachers / Nancy Mamlin.
    p. cm. — (What works for special-needs learners)
  Includes bibliographical references and index.
  ISBN 978-1-4625-0306-3 (pbk.) — ISBN 978-1-4625-0307-0 (hardcover)
  1. Special education teachers—Training of—United States.   2. Special education—
Study and teaching—United States.   I. Title.
  LC3969.45.M36 2012
  371.9′043—dc23

                                     2011044961

To Richard Dever and Dennis Knapczyk,
who first taught me how to teach

About the Author

Nancy Mamlin, PhD, is Associate Professor of Special Education and Coordinator of the Learning Disabilities Program at the H. M. Michaux, Jr. School of Education, North Carolina Central University. Dr. Mamlin received her initial teacher preparation at Indiana University in the areas of intellectual and emotional disabilities. She taught in Palo Alto, California, and Pittsburgh, Pennsylvania, before earning her master's degree from the University of Maryland. After teaching in Rockville, Maryland, for 2 years, she returned to school and earned a doctorate in special education (with a concentration in learning disabilities) from the University of Maryland in 1995. Dr. Mamlin has been a teacher educator at Appalachian State University and North Carolina Central University, and has prepared teacher candidates by working with them in their student teaching and internship settings. She has focused her research on general and special education teachers and what they need to know in order to work with their students who have special education needs.

Preface

Whenever you are asked if you can do a job, tell 'em,
"Certainly I can!" Then get busy and find out how to do it.
—THEODORE ROOSEVELT

When I was approached by the series editors, Karen Harris and Steve Graham, about contributing this volume, I immediately said "yes." I've been involved in special education for decades and in special education teacher preparation since I began my master's degree in 1988. Though my advanced degrees are in learning disabilities, most of my work—teaching, research, and service—has revolved around the lives of teachers and how we might best develop new teachers and support and enhance the skills of practicing teachers. I was somewhat surprised, as I began research on this book, to discover that the last book written on the preparation of special education teachers (and perhaps the only book of its kind) was published in 1974. There are several books about how to prepare teachers in general (e.g., Darling-Hammond, 2006), but special education has some unique features that make preparing teachers for this field worthy of special consideration.

This book is intended for use primarily by individuals involved in teacher preparation, or preparing to be teacher educators. It could be used as a primary or secondary text for doctoral students in teacher education, and as a reference for staff development professionals and policymakers. I hope that it can provide teacher educators with a way to think about and evaluate their programs. Secondary audiences would include practicing teacher educators, university and school system leaders, teachers, staff development professionals, researchers, and educational policymakers. This book expands on the Council for Exceptional Children (2009) standards for teacher education by providing some specifics on how to go about meeting the standards. My approach to writing this has been to pull together relevant and current research, and to present a framework for preparing excellent special educators. I hope that readers find this information useful in whatever area of special education teacher preparation they are engaged.

Acknowledgments

First and foremost, I would like to acknowledge the encouragement, advice, and friendship of Karen Harris and Steve Graham. For over 20 years they have guided me through graduate school, various jobs, moves, and projects, providing valuable leadership for me at critical times.

I would also like to thank the special education faculty at Appalachian State University, and indeed the entire faculty of the Department of Language, Reading, and Exceptionalities, who witnessed my development as a teacher educator. I look forward to continued collaboration with you all. Additionally, the Hubbard Center for Faculty Development at Appalachian offered me countless resources and support as a teacher educator and gave me a place to explore and talk about the job of a university faculty member. I also express my appreciation to my colleagues in the Department of Special Education at North Carolina Central University, who have provided me with the space and place to get the vast majority of this book completed.

Finally, I must acknowledge the important and unwavering support of my family. My parents, Harry and Mary Lee Mamlin, were my first teachers, and have continued to be good sounding boards for my ideas. My husband, Ron Cole, has been consistently supportive of my career goals, and luckily lets me play music with him even though he's better at it than I am. I won't attempt the impossible task of listing all my family members who have provided support, many of whom are involved in education or child welfare—suffice it to say that you all set high standards and continue to inspire me.

Contents

Preparing Effective
Special Education Teachers

CHAPTER 1

A Framework for Teacher Education in Special Education

Teacher Education Matters

> We shouldn't try to do something better until we first
> determine if we should do it at all.
> —DWIGHT D. EISENHOWER

As in other fields of teacher training, special education is undergoing significant changes. In addition to the growing need to supply the nation with sufficient numbers of teachers to meet the demand for special educational services, there is an increasing emphasis on improving the quality of the teacher-training process and product. Teacher preparation programs, like the personnel they train, are being held accountable for their methods through the effects they produce; hence, the trend toward competency-based teacher certification. (Thiagarajan, Semmel, & Semmel, 1974, p. 3)

This quotation is from a book written over 35 years ago, *Instructional Development for Training Teachers of Exceptional Children: A Sourcebook*. In the book, teacher trainers were given guidelines for how to train candidates for positions in special education. While some of the techniques in those pages might, in the 21st century, seem dated, or even inadequate, most of what they wrote is still relevant today. Teacher trainers were told to determine what instructional materials might be required, and who the learners were (meaning candidates). They were also guided toward task-analyzing the teaching process, and how to specify instructional objectives.

Then, in the second part of the book, readers were taught about construction of criterion-referenced tests, methods of instruction, mastery learning, self-instructional formats, and even some computer-based formats of training. In the final two parts of the book, special education teacher educators were given guidelines on how to develop and disseminate what has been developed to complete the process of teacher training. Over 35 years later, this remains the only book to have addressed special education teacher education, even though research in the field has continued, and journals such as *Teacher Education and Special Education* publish up-to-date research and descriptions of excellent programs. So, what do we know about the status of special education teacher preparation in the 21st century?

It is difficult to open a journal, or even a newspaper, these days without seeing a mention of the current shortage of teachers, especially in the areas of mathematics, sciences, and special education. These shortages are not new, nor is there any real sign of their abating soon. At the same time, in the current economic crisis, it is equally common to read of layoffs, cutbacks of services, pay cuts, and so forth. In the face of these circumstances, encouraging candidates to enter a field they have little experience in can be difficult. Even with current, hopefully short term, cutbacks, there still seem to be too few special education teachers produced, either by institutions of higher education (universities) or alternate means.

The research on teacher shortages, though, is problematic, as it is confounded with issues of definitions of high quality, certification, and what counts as attrition. Some researchers count leaving a particular job or district as attrition, whereas others may count as attribution an actual change from the field of education. Therefore, a teacher who simply moves to a new school district, and takes another special education teaching job, might be counted as a "leaver." Likewise, individuals who leave the classroom for jobs in administration, or to pursue an advanced degree, may be counted as leaving the field in one study but not in another. In my career, I might have been counted as a leaver several times: when I left my first job to move to another state, when I left that state and teaching position to go to graduate school, and when I left my job after graduate school to return for my PhD studies. However, I have never left the field, even though I have left the classroom. At any rate, it is not clear that the problems are as severe as presented in some places, but it does seem clear that there is, in fact, a shortage (Boe, 2006). It is not within the scope of this book to address these issues directly, but they surely impact how the task of preparing teachers should be (and will be) approached.

Due to the prevailing shortages of special education teachers, special education teacher educators face pressures from schools, universities, state education departments, and the public in general to turn out more and better teachers more quickly. How do we work with these tensions and competing interests of excellent preparation and rapid preparation? What are the factors that help develop good teachers? How do we prepare best? Even with the rush to quickly prepare teachers—the focus needs to be on doing that *well*, regardless of the time it takes.

Currently, there are various avenues described in the literature for approaching special education teacher education: undergraduate preparation, fifth-year programs, graduate-level preparation (including Master of Arts in Teaching [MAT] degrees), a possible need for general education certification first, classes offered on a traditional campus, online instruction, on-the-job learning, regional centers, and more. That said, how do we work with these tensions as well as competing interests of excellent preparation and rapid preparation? The purpose of this book is to discuss features of teacher education programs that produce excellent teachers, realizing that the same goals can be accomplished in many different ways. I intend to describe the important features we need to include in our courses and programs. These features of excellent preparation should be considered no matter how the candidates come to us. Simply put, the job of the special education teacher educator is to produce excellent special education teachers. To do that, we must consider what needs to be part of their education and then provide it.

This chapter lays out what is known about effective teacher education programs in general education, and discusses how these features may appear in special education teacher preparation (Brownell, Ross, Colón, & McCallum, 2003; Darling-Hammond, 2006). This chapter also addresses what sets special education teacher education apart from general teacher education. What is "special," in other words, about our work? The literature on the nature and needs of the shortage of special education teachers helps inform the chapter, as well as what may set special education apart from other areas that may also be experiencing shortages (Duffy & Forgan, 2005). Finally, there will be a brief discussion of two sets of standards which inform teacher education. The Council for Exceptional Children's (CEC, 2009) standards for special educators are a major resource that informs teacher preparation practices. The other set of standards for teacher educators are general standards for teacher education from the Association of Teacher Educators (ATE, 2007).

EFFECTIVE TEACHER EDUCATION IN GENERAL EDUCATION

While there is research that addresses teacher preparation for general education teachers (Cochran-Smith & Zeichner, 2005; Darling-Hammond & Baratz-Snowden, 2005; Lampert, 2001), it is not a well-established area of high-quality research. Israel (2009) suggested that there is likely an assumption that teacher preparation should be intuitive to teachers. There is historical precedence for this. Before the establishment of normal schools, individuals merely had to be good students in order to teach. Now, university preparation of teachers is the norm, but how candidates are taught in universities is not well studied. That said, there are position and policy papers, if not a large body of research, regarding general education teacher education.

Reviewing the literature, there are aspects of general teacher education that can be generalized across specialty areas, including special education. Effective teacher education programs in general education have been described by Brownell and colleagues (2003) and Darling-Hammond (2006) and include the following features:

1. Faculty have a coherent, common, and clear vision of good teaching.
2. Faculty have developed standards for ensuring quality teaching by the candidates.
3. There is a blending of theory, disciplinary knowledge, and subject-specific pedagogical knowledge and practice.
4. Faculty use an active pedagogy that employs modeling and promotes reflection.
5. The curriculum is grounded in knowledge of child and adolescent development, learning, social contexts, and subject matter.
6. Faculty use case study methods, teacher research, performance assessments, and portfolio evaluation. Learning is applied to real problems.
7. There are carefully crafted and extended clinical experiences.
8. The curriculum focuses on meeting the needs of a diverse student population and contains explicit strategies to help candidates confront their beliefs/assumptions about people different from themselves.
9. Collaboration is used as a vehicle for building a professional community, and strong relationships, common knowledge, and shared beliefs link school-based and university-based faculty.
10. Well-defined standards of practice and performance are used to guide and evaluate coursework/clinical work.

General education teacher preparation, therefore, can provide guidance for various specialty areas in education, including special education. The various standards can serve as guideposts for what to include in programs, at a minimum, to help candidates become teachers in any field. In the subsequent chapters of this book, the ideals and standards for general teacher education will help inform what special education teacher education should look like.

No Dream Denied

Spooner (2005) enumerated what to look for in quality teacher preparation, naming the six dimensions from *No Dream Denied* (National Commission on Teaching and America's Future, 2003):

1. Careful recruitment and selection of candidates.
2. Strong academic preparation for teaching, including deep knowledge of subjects to be taught, and firm understanding of how students learn.
3. Extensive clinical practice to develop effective teaching skills, including an ability to teach specific content effectively, at specific grade levels, to diverse students.
4. Entry-level teaching support through residencies and mentored induction.
5. Modern learning technologies that are embedded in academic preparation, clinical practice, induction, and ongoing professional development.
6. Assessment of teacher preparation programs' effectiveness.

Each of these dimensions raises questions for special education. Many special education teacher preparation programs are hampered in their ability to recruit and select candidates carefully. In many cases, the programs are small, and might be under pressure to increase enrollment by lowering or ignoring standards. Another situation that arises are candidates coming to programs who have already been hired by schools as special education teachers on an emergency or provisional basis, and nearby programs that have an ethical obligation to train them to be good special education teachers. Having a strong academic preparation for teaching is certainly a worthy goal, but having a deep understanding of all subjects to be taught might be more unattainable. Special educators should have a firm understanding of how students learn, which in fact might be considered foundational to their content knowledge. The third factor noted by Spooner (2005), providing extensive clinical practice, is something that is difficult to argue with in principle, but also can be difficult to fulfill since special educators are often licensed over a wide range of grades, or types of disability. These issues will be directly addressed in other chapters of the book.

Continuing to examine this list (National Commission on Teaching and America's Future, 2003; Spooner, 2005), and how it relates to special education teacher preparation, we should keep in mind that the new teachers who are entering the field will still require support, and we can work closely with school districts to help support these new teachers in their first several years. As technology becomes more a part of our daily lives, and options expand, training programs are in a position to reach teachers (former candidates) and continue the teaching and mentoring process. Finally, to determine if we are doing what we set out to do, we must assess our programs. These issues are discussed in more detail later in this book.

EFFECTIVE TEACHER EDUCATION IN SPECIAL EDUCATION

While there is guidance available about general education teacher education, special education teacher education is not an established area of inquiry (Brownell et al., 2003; Israel, 2009; Leko, 2008). Israel (2009) provided the following basic definition of special education teacher education, whether it originates at a university or is based in a school district: Special education teacher education involves introducing preservice or inservice teachers to the content and pedagogical tools necessary to teach students with disabilities effectively. The inherent complexities of teacher education are magnified when it comes to special education teacher education (Israel, 2009). At this point there is no solid synthesis of available programs and their features. The focus of programs varies according to age and grade levels and categories of disability covered, which may alter significantly what programs cover.

Further complicating matters is that we currently find ourselves in a crisis situation regarding preparing special education teachers quickly in order to get them into classrooms where they are needed. There is little time to truly investigate what method or methods of preparation would be preferable. Instead, universities find themselves under pressure from state departments of public instruction to produce teachers with as few "roadblocks" as possible. Universities may have a different viewpoint, and see these roadblocks as necessary to the degree program, the school, college, or university vision, or best practice. States have established various methods for producing licensed teachers, ranging from full degree programs to methods that require no coursework whatsoever, beyond the possession of a bachelor's degree.

Indeed, despite the wide variety of options for candidates, the majority of special educators are prepared, at least in part, in traditional university programs. This indicates that the attention to alternative routes may be blown out of proportion—or overcovered—in the literature and overshadow the larger issues of special education teacher education. At this point, the literature available points to the advantages of a coherent program (see above). The literature is less clear as to whether "fast-track" licensure, or taking courses at a variety of universities to meet discreet standards, will lead to excellent special education teachers. At the very least, preparation approaches should include the qualities addressed in this book.

Alternative Routes to Licensure

Given that there are numerous routes to licensure for special education teachers, it is important to briefly consider conditions for success in alternate routes. Several have been identified in the literature, including the following, identified by Bergeron, Larson, Prest, Dumas-Hopper, and Wenhart (2005): communication, use of cohorts, field experiences, partnerships with local education agencies (LEAs), practical experiences, and use of technology. The optimal size of a cohort or class size for creating community was described as "small" by Beck and Kosnik (2006), by which they meant 25–80 candidates, dividing these groups into even smaller cohorts for subject areas, practicum clusters, and so forth. These conditions very closely mirror the conditions for success in teacher preparation in general. While these features have been suggested as conditions for success, it is unclear how many alternative routes have how many of these features in place, and to what extent.

Given the wide variability, the jury is still out regarding the efficacy of alternate routes in teacher preparation. Since there are so many variations on what is possible, it becomes difficult to draw strong conclusions. There is also an argument to be made that, since candidates for traditional routes may differ from those for alternate routes, comparison of the candidates is probably not useful. The question, in any case, is whether or not candidates are being prepared to take on the role of special education teacher at the end of their training. Whether you are in the position, therefore, of providing support to candidates taking a traditional undergraduate or graduate program, or candidates taking an alternate route, or some combination of those scenarios, the recommendations in these pages should be useful. It is beyond the scope of this book to address the wisdom or efficacy of these paths to licensure, though it is my bias/belief that preparation in a university program is preferable.

Features of Special Education Programs

Brownell and her colleagues (2003) completed a review of features of special education programs described in the literature. These, which I discuss in more detail in the following chapters, include the following attributes:

Maintaining a Positivist or Constructivist Orientation toward Learning/Teaching

Effective programs may emphasize one of these orientations or have a blended approach. Whichever orientation is taken by the program, a strong competency-based approach to teacher education assumes that a specific set of knowledge and skills exists and should be disseminated to students. This is not to say that orientations and emphases cannot shift and change over time. What is important is that there is a strong, well-articulated, and defensible approach to special education teacher education. (See Chapter 2.)

Crafting Extensive Field Experiences That Are Well Supervised, Incorporate Practices Acquired in Courses, and Provide Links between Theory and Practice

This area of teacher preparation has gotten much attention, and rightly so. It has long been recognized that field experiences are where candidates are given the opportunities to practice skills learned in classrooms. At the same time, this is the area that is most difficult to control, since there are myriad factors beyond the control of the university or entity making the placement. (See Chapter 3.)

Focus on Inclusion

Since the late 1980s, students with disabilities have been increasingly likely to be educated alongside their general education peers in inclusive settings. As of 2006, 95% of students 6 to 21 years old served under the Individuals with Disabilities Education Improvement Act of 2004 (IDEIA) have been enrolled in a regular school. Furthermore, over 80% of students receiving services are educated at least part of the day in general education classrooms: 53.7% spend less than 21% of their time outside the general classroom, and 23.7% spend 21–60% of their time outside the general classroom (U.S. Department of Education, National Center for Education Statistics, 2010). Therefore, effective special education teacher educators emphasize education about inclusive practices. (See Chapter 5.)

Diversity Education

In addition to inclusion of students with various ability levels, special education teacher educators also need to help candidates increase their knowledge about cultural diversity. Not surprisingly, increasing diversity in the schools has received a lot of attention from the general public. Current estimates are that by 2020 nearly 40% of students will be members of a historically underrepresented culture (Kewal Ramani, Gilbertson, Fox, & Provasnik, 2007). However, teachers, at this point at least, still tend to be female and white. Regardless of the cultural background of the special education teachers, they must be prepared to teach in a cultural context that is very likely to be different from the one in which they were educated. (See Chapter 5.)

Working Together

Special education programs need to include information about collaboration, including collaboration between teachers, between schools and teachers, and among cohorts of candidates. Coursework for students about collaboration with families and professionals is likely going to be an important part of accomplishing this goal. While the area of collaboration is recognized in special education as an important part of the job, the concept of collaboration is not as likely to be covered in general education preparation programs. It then becomes incumbent on the special education faculty to communicate with general education faculty about the need to collaborate. It also becomes the job of the candidates to learn leadership skills as well, as special educators are often in the position of being "lead collaborator" with a variety of people. Teachers need to communicate regularly with parents and work with them as team members for the benefit of the student. Special education teachers may also find themselves in the position at times of supervising one or more paraprofessionals. Finally, they must collaborate with general educators to get information about the general curriculum and collaborate on appropriate modifications and accommodations for students. (See Chapter 5.)

Evaluating the Impact of Teacher Education Programs through a Variety of Assessment Methods

Effective programs, including special education programs, are continually evaluated and adjustments are made where needed. Special education teacher educators take into account candidate feedback, employer feedback, and peer feedback. They also pay attention to changing requirements and changing circumstances when determining needed changes. (See Chapter 6.)

DIFFERENCES BETWEEN TEACHER EDUCATION IN GENERAL AND SPECIAL EDUCATION

As stated earlier, there is a body of literature regarding the preparation of general education teachers, and we can extrapolate from that literature to a certain extent for the purposes of preparing special education teachers. The question, then, is whether special education is different in any way in terms of teacher preparation. If it is different, why is there not a body of literature and research about it? One answer is that special education is a relatively young field, whether using 1974 (passage of Public Law 94-142, the Education of Handicapped Children Act) or 1922 (founding of CEC) or another date as a starting point. Education for the general population has been addressed in a more systematic way for longer than that, and teachers have been trained to teach general education populations since a much earlier time. So, the relative newness of the field may be one explanation as to why there has been but one book (Thiagarajan et al., 1974) written about how to prepare special education teachers. There is literature available in journals, but it has not yet been pulled together in a coherent way for the purpose of guiding special education teacher education practice. That is another goal of this volume.

An alternative explanation for the lack of research may be that preparing special education teachers is no different from preparing general education teachers. At its most basic, this is true. However, Duffy and Forgan (2005) pointed out several factors that make special education teacher preparation unique. Special educators do, indeed, have special knowledge that prepares them to provide specialized services for their students, their students' families, and other professionals. These areas include (1) IDEIA legislation; (2) forms of assessment; (3) medical information; (4) due process, individualized education plans (IEPs), and referrals; (5) instructional strategies and diversity of accommodations; (6) complex teacher roles; (7) collaborating with general educators, parents, and paraprofessionals; and (8) cultural diversity issues. The final two items on this list were addressed previously, so will not be repeated here. The remaining six items, though, are explained briefly below:

IDEIA Legislation

IDEIA legislation is perhaps the most obvious area making special education teacher education and teachers different from general education teacher education and teachers. Knowledge of the current law (IDEIA, 2004) is critical, and as it approaches regular reauthorizations, special education teacher educators need to make themselves aware of the issues involved and provide feedback to appropriate parties on potential changes. Further, they must convey this knowledge to candidates and help them understand how to use it in practice.

Assessment Practices

Special education teachers are often called upon to administer individual achievement tests to students who have or are suspected of having disabilities. They are also responsible for interpreting tests for parents, teachers, and others who may have an interest in the results. Additionally, they may be in a position of developing both formative and summative assessments for their students. Special education teacher educators, therefore, must stay updated on assessment practices and be willing to spend the time it takes to help candidates become proficient in administering and choosing the appropriate tools. Special education teachers also must be expert in modifying or otherwise making accessible teacher-made assessments. They need a deep understanding of how to allow students to "show what they know."

Medical Issues

Special education teachers are more likely than other teachers to deal with a host of medical issues, including administering or monitoring medication their students take, and tracking behavioral or other changes resulting from the medication. They may be in the position of providing first aid such as in the case of seizure disorders, and may at times have to provide more specialized care for certain students.

Due Process, IEPs, and Referrals

While general educators have responsibilities for participation in the IEP process, and they are often the ones who initiate referrals for special education, it is often up to the special educator to help guide the process. The special educator is expected to be up to date as procedures change, and to help others in their school understand those changes. For example, as more schools and LEAs move toward using response to intervention (RTI) to assess students suspected of having a learning disability, the special educator must understand fully the various components involved in the process. Special education teacher educators likewise need to be up to date on these procedures and help candidates understand them, as well as on controversies that may exist and pitfalls to avoid.

Instructional Strategies and Diversity of Accommodations

While general educators certainly understand instructional strategies, special educators are expected to have a wider array of such strategies at their disposal. Since special educators work with the students who are not typical learners, they tend to have more experience with and knowledge of a variety of methods. Similarly, since special educators encounter students with a wide range of needs, and possibly quite unique needs, they need to be excellent problem solvers and at times be quite creative in how accommodations are made for their students. In his meta-analyses of what works for students with learning disabilities, for example, Lee Swanson and colleagues (Swanson & Hoskyn, 1998; Swanson & Sachse-Lee, 2000) identified strategies instruction as a positive influence on academic achievement.

Complex Teacher Roles

As has already been noted, special education teachers may take on a variety of "teacher roles," which may vary over the course of an individual teacher's career. These teachers may be lead, or primary teacher for their students, may co-teach with general educators, may collaborate with other professionals (physical, occupational, or other therapists; speech/language pathologists; or medical professionals), may have paraprofessionals whom they supervise, and/or may be consultants to other teachers. They need to be prepared to work effectively at any point along the continuum of placements available to students. They also need to understand these various arrangements and be able to advocate for their students so that their students have the best learning situation for their needs. As special education teacher roles continue to evolve, both teachers and teacher educators need to be able to take on new roles and responsibilities, as well as be informed enough to articulate the appropriateness of new roles and responsibilities.

NATURE OF THE SPECIAL EDUCATION TEACHER SHORTAGE

In education, the most common areas of teacher shortage have historically been math, science, and special education. Math and science teacher shortages might be partially explained by the job opportunities outside of education. Special education, on the other hand, does not have that "excuse." So why is there such a shortage? One explanation might be that most potential candidates are not aware of special education as a career opportunity. It is likely that potential teachers were not recipients of special education in their own schooling. College students may choose another education major with the stated objective of helping students who struggle, and might be unaware of special education as a field. The onus falls, in my opinion, on faculty members at universities to speak to potential education majors about special education as a field. Duffy and Forgan (2005) mentioned several strategies, including "grow your own," recruiting candidates from non-shortage areas, and mentoring to retain. Special education programs can use university resources to contact college students who are "undeclared" or "undecided" majors. Directly contacting them with an invitation to consider special education can increase the numbers of candidates who are in preparation programs, and eventually teaching.

Sun, Bender, and Fore (2003) provided an example from Georgia of a web-based certification program developed in an effort to increase the supply of special education teachers in the state. They found that having a web-based option tended to increase enrollment. They provided cautions for universities about how to go about starting an online program and how to do it well. It is also up to professional organizations to advocate for better working conditions, realistic job expectations, and good laws protecting students, families, and teachers. While this book focuses on quality special education teacher education, some of the same approaches can be applied to retention and advocacy, so might be of interest to those audiences as well.

Another explanation for the small numbers of students pursuing degrees in special education is that as a field special education may have a "bad" reputation: Potential candidates may have heard of difficult students and "too much" paperwork, and might be concerned about not having "their own class." More and more, though, these are features of general education as well, given the Elementary and Secondary Education Act (ESEA, recently known as No Child Left Behind [NCLB]) and other requirements. It is up to special education teacher educators to better explain the job of a special educator, dispel myths, and assure candidates they can be equipped to deal with the complexities of the job.

Retaining Good Special Educators

While various strategies might increase the number of new special education teachers, the next task, retaining them, belongs primarily to the schools (Billingsley, 2005). According to the CEC (Duffy & Forgan, 2005), within the first 5 years, four out of ten teachers leave the field of special education. By 2005 over 200,000 new special educators were needed. Cook and Boe (2007), however, suggested that teacher shortages appear to be more a result of inadequate supply to the field than of attrition issues. According to Duffy and Forgan (2005), *Education Week* reported that 98% of districts fell short of filling positions. Boyer and Mainzer (2003) stated that in the last 10 years of the 20th century, when there was an increase in students identified with disabilities by 30%, the increase in teaching positions rose by just 11%. Special education teacher education can help change these statistics by equipping special education teachers well, following up in initial years to mentor formally or informally, and help candidates find their voices as advocates for their profession.

While trying to limit attrition, we should also be cautious about being too disparaging of leavers or transfers. People may leave to pursue more education, and if they proceed through to a doctoral program, they may ultimately contribute to increasing the special education teacher pool. Some may leave temporarily to start a family, in which case they are counted in some studies as leavers, and may or may not be counted as returners. Some may leave for positions in administration or in general education and can still have an important, positive impact on students receiving special education services. What is concerning in attrition studies, though, is when teachers who leave note lack of preparation as a reason (Billingsley, 2004; Mastropieri, 2001; Miller, Brownell, & Smith, 1999; Whitaker, 2001). This factor clearly falls within the purview of special education teacher education.

Who Leaves and Who Stays?

In reviewing data from the U.S. Department of Education, Office of Special Education Programs (OSEP), Boe (2006) found an increase over time in both the number of students identified with disabilities *and* increases in the number of teacher positions. These teacher positions, according to these data, were *mostly filled* with fully certified teachers. Boe still cited problems of quality and quantity. As he noted, while the quantitative data are problematic, it is clear that a real shortage exists.

Quality or the lack thereof is also difficult to judge. Boe (2006) defined it simply as appropriate or lack of appropriate certification. One difficulty with this way of looking at quality is the wide range of what is considered to be "inappropriate certification." For example, a teacher might be considered inappropriately certified if he or she is teaching high school special education with an elementary special education certificate. A second teacher hired for the same job who does not have any education degree at all is similarly counted as "inappropriately certified." Presumably, hiring the first teacher would result in higher-quality instruction. Special education students are typically not sorted according to disability label for instruction, yet many states certify teachers according to disability label. This can also lead to special education teachers who are technically "inappropriately certified" yet have the necessary skills and training to do an effective job.

Gehrke and Murri (2006) looked at the issue of retention from a different perspective: discovering why special education teachers remain in the field. They found that teachers who stayed in special education were those who were resourceful and resilient in advocating for their students and programs. These teachers still expressed frustration around issues of inclusion and curriculum, however.

Writing about attrition of teachers, Billingsley (2004) discovered that individuals who had higher NTE scores (National Teachers' Exam, now the PRAXIS series) were twice as likely to leave as those who received lower scores. Similarly, teachers who received additional degrees (master's and beyond) were more likely to leave. These results are not really surprising, and they are related. Teachers may obtain further education for the purpose of leaving the classroom (to administration or to higher education). Likewise, teachers who score well on standardized tests are more likely to meet admission requirements for these degree programs. Billingsley found that the likely leavers were younger and had less experience, were uncertified, had higher test scores, or left for personal reasons. In conclusion, regardless of the reason for shortages or for attrition, it is clear that we need more and better strategies to attract individuals into the field of special education, give them the tools they need, support them as they learn, and mentor them as they begin their careers.

OUR ROLE AS TEACHER EDUCATORS

As teacher educators, we have at least five areas of professional identity: teacher, scholar, collaborator, learner, and leader. Cochran-Smith (2003) identified three traditional areas of teacher educators' work: teacher education, research and inquiry into teaching and learning, and policy analysis as it relates to education and social justice. In many cases we notice a blurring of these roles. Guskey (2000), in his book about evaluating professional development, provided the following steps to guide school districts in designing professional development, which can be applied to teacher education and teacher education preparation as well: (1) begin with a clear statement of purposes and goals, which need to be examined and evaluated; (2) ensure that the goals are worthwhile; and (3) determine how the goals can be assessed. The following chapters address these in the context of preparing special education teachers.

At the University of Wisconsin–Madison (UWM), Zeichner and Conklin (2005) developed a series of graduate courses in teacher education: supervision/mentoring preservice teachers, analysis of pertinent policy issues, teacher professional development, and reflective practices in teacher education. It was reported that most UWM doctoral students did not take these courses. Zeichner and Conklin suggested that these students saw their role as teacher educator as a means of financing doctoral studies related to their major focus area and considered teacher education to be of secondary importance. This may lead to problems in learning to be a teacher as a candidate in a research-intensive university. Many faculty have taught only in this type of university. It is seen by some as superior, and there is a bias toward working there. Doctoral students are not typically exposed to learning and teaching in smaller institutions. In my own case, I attended research-intensive universities exclusively and only when I got a job after graduating was I at an institution that placed more emphasis on teaching. Whether we are at a major university or a smaller institution, if we find ourselves in the role of a teacher educator, we need to take that role seriously and encourage excellent special education candidates and teachers to explore various options for becoming excellent teacher educators.

What Do Special Education Teacher Educators Think?

In his keynote address at the Teacher Education Division (TED) of the CEC in 2007, Meyen reported on a survey of the TED membership and discussed the results in several areas. These results are useful as we consider how to best frame special education teacher education. He found that the major changes (roadblocks, challenges) that have hindered teacher education in special education were unfunded mandates, an overemphasis on bureaucratic processes, and the NCLB highly qualified approach. He suggested that we strategically recruit into special education teacher education and offered several recommendations for the organization (TED as well as the parent organization CEC) to pursue.

The overarching recommendation he offered was to improve teacher education. He also suggested to the membership that they continue to pursue advocacy and provide national leadership on issues. The areas of concern noted by Meyen included research on teacher education, issues surrounding certification and licensure, definitions of highly qualified teachers and other NCLB issues, and, finally, recruitment of individuals to the profession of teacher education. As special education teacher educators become more involved in policy and address issues noted by Meyen as well as the reauthorizations of ESEA (currently NCLB), the higher education act, and IDEIA, the profession of special education teacher educator is improved and becomes more capable of doing its job and attracting more people to its ranks.

So, what else might be needed for teacher educators to do their jobs better and to address these issues in the field, particularly the field of special education? Meyen, in his research, found that the following conditions need to be in place to ensure effective special education teacher educators. First, quality faculty colleagues are important. This may be an issue in many universities, as special education faculty might be part of a larger department, school, or college which may not have the same goals, outcomes, or perspectives as special education.

Special education teacher educators might feel isolated if they are the one person representing the field of special education at their university. In those cases, it is important for the faculty member to seek out people within the university to collaborate with, as well as other special education faculty in other institutions. Special education faculty, like the candidates they are training, also may find themselves in the position of educating their colleagues about their roles and responsibilities.

The second area of concern noted by Meyen (2007) was professional preparation of teacher educators. Doctoral programs typically focus on an area of disability rather than special education teacher education. However, faculty who do not work in research-intensive universities are primarily working as teacher educators. How we are prepared to fulfill this critical role is an understudied area (Israel, 2009). In a special issue of *Teacher Education and Special Education* (Johnson & Bauer, 2003), on the study of special education leadership, one group of authors suggested a part-time EdD program for preparing special education teacher educators (Evans, Andrews, Miller, & Smith, 2003).

In the same issue, Pion, Smith, and Tyler (2003) noted that, as with K–12 teachers, there are more faculty vacancies than graduates of doctoral programs, and there is therefore a persistent unmet demand. This is logical, of course, since there is a shortage of special education teachers, and the supply of available faculty functions like a funnel in the following manner: Special education teacher educators come from the ranks of special education teachers, which is already a small pool. Teacher educators are the subset of special education teachers who want to pursue doctoral degrees, and who then want to pursue careers in universities. Also, since there are many more universities that prepare teachers than grant doctoral degrees, this adds to the supply/demand issue. Smith, Pion, Tyler, and Gilmore (2003) found that more than a third of searches in special education teacher education were failed searches. For example, in California, the six schools with doctoral degrees in special education graduated about six students per year, and only two per year pursued faculty positions. This shortage also naturally affects school districts' ability to provide appropriate education for all students.

Israel (2009) found just 18 studies that related to either preparation of teacher educators or the skills/competencies of teacher educators. It should be noted that this review represented all teacher educators, not just special education teacher educators, and much of the research was international, which further complicates conclusions for special education teacher education. A persistent issue with teacher education faculty is their lack of identification with their role as teacher educators (Israel, 2009). Faculty are more likely to identify with their discipline or research. Like the candidates they are preparing, teacher educators have a range of roles. This is highlighted by responsibilities which come with different Carnegie classifications. In any faculty position, there are additional parts of the job beyond teacher preparation—research and service, for example. Other roles may include working with novice teachers, collaborating with school districts, and facilitating policy changes. All of these are important, and can inform your role as a teacher educator. Unfortunately, the field has largely ignored the preparation of and institutional supports for teacher educators (Cochran-Smith, 2003). The overarching issue is that teacher educators and researchers have yet to identify best practices adequately.

In her research, Israel (2009) discussed how special education teacher educators were prepared. She found diversity among doctoral programs. Not all were focused on teacher education, and few had it as a line of inquiry. She concluded that future special education teacher educators should be provided with experiences that immerse them in the practices of teacher educators (Zeichner & Conklin, 2005), just as we try, as teacher educators, to immerse candidates in field experiences and practice prior to their entering the field. Logically, doctoral students would benefit from directed experiences that prepare them for their future role as teacher educators (Cochran-Smith, 2003). There are similarities between educating teacher educators and educating teachers in that it is difficult to link outcomes of students directly to the practice of the educator (or teacher educator), but making those connections may be important.

A final finding by Meyen (2007) was that responders to his survey found involvement in associations to be important to their success. Of course, his respondents were those who were already members of professional associations, so the sample was biased in that direction. This is still an important consideration for special education teacher educators, though, given the potential isolation of special education faculty noted above. Involvement in professional associations can be a very important part of maintaining one's grounding and sanity. Involvement also gives members access to journals, websites, blogs, and more. Information is made available to members on upcoming legislation, as well as opportunities to be involved as the legislation is being drafted.

Meyen's research also uncovered what responders felt hindered their effectiveness as special education teacher educators. These included the conditions of a heavy workload, insufficient research time, and an insufficient appreciation for teacher education. In most cases, special education should be expected to be a smaller program than general education in terms of candidates prepared. But special education teacher education might then draw attention as a small program and thereby be in danger of being cut. Faculty need to be prepared to explain and defend their programs. Policies in Meyen's survey that were noted as hindering progress in special education teacher education included unfunded and underfunded legislation (notably IDEIA as well as NCLB), the failure of reforms to include disabilities, and the issues surrounding NCLB and standardized testing. Responders to Meyen also indicated what they wanted for special education teacher education. Basically, special education teacher educators desired more collaboration in teacher preparation, more collaboration in K–12 education, and more effort or emphasis on inclusion.

REQUIREMENTS FOR SPECIAL EDUCATION TEACHERS

Teacher education requirements have been seen as a barrier to entering the profession. In response to these complaints, we have seen an increased interest in eliminating or changing some of these barriers. However, this is not without cost to candidates as well as programs. For example, North Carolina had as an entry requirement to teacher education that candidates have a 2.5 grade-point average (GPA) out of a possible 4.0. This has been changed, and universities now have the option of eliminating that requirement. However, a 2.5 GPA is still required for licensure, and in many cases for graduation, so students may find themselves being able to enter teacher education programs, but not exit with a license if they were unable to bridge the gap between their entering GPA and the 2.5 required for licensure. Lessening restrictions, however they are operationalized, is in response to the basic problem: Children keep showing up at schools, and they need teachers.

Special education is different from other fields, since changing licensing requirements in other fields would not have the potential to eliminate federally mandated services. For example, changing licensing requirements so that middle school teachers do not need to specialize in a content area, but are more broadly prepared (like their elementary education counterparts), would not cause middle school students to stop receiving an education. Or, to take a more extreme case, a state could decide that physical education was no longer a required part of the curriculum, thereby eliminating the need for physical education teacher education in universities in that state. However, if special education licensure was determined to be unnecessary, special education students in the state might not be able to receive FAPE (free and appropriate public education). So, as long as there is legislation mandating special education, there will be a need for special education teachers, and therefore preparation programs. Teacher educators must fully understand how these evolving issues relate to preservice teacher education and licensure as their instruction influences teacher effectiveness (Nougaret, Scruggs, & Mastropieri, 2005; Sindelar & Rosenberg, 2000).

CEC STANDARDS

The CEC provides a definition of a well-prepared special education teacher (2003, 2009). The standards include a recognition that professional preparation occurs along a continuum, from initial preparation, to induction and mentoring, through to continual professional growth. The focus of this book is primarily on how to accomplish the first step of that process, and how this may lead to the next two steps of entry to and continuation in the profession.

An important initial statement from CEC is that beginning special education teachers hold a bachelor's degree from an accredited institution at a minimum.

This idea conflicts with some proposals by states to allow community colleges to provide teacher preparation. If states were to be successful in these attempts, teachers prepared there might not be able to be licensed in other states, to say nothing of the lessening of their professional status.

CEC standards for well-prepared special educators state that teachers have mastered appropriate core academic subject matter, the knowledge and skills in the CEC Common Core, and an appropriate area of specialization. Pedagogy, or teaching skill, is noted as the actual content of special education. Special education knowledge, in other words, is not about knowledge of any particular academic content that K–12 students might be studying, but is the knowledge of how learning occurs, and what good teaching entails. CEC expects special educators to know subject matter sufficiently to collaborate with general educators, in teaching or co-teaching the subject matter, and designing appropriate learning and performance accommodations and modifications. They note, however, that if a special educator is going to assume sole responsibility for teaching a core academic subject, they must have a solid knowledge base sufficient for students to meet state standards. This is more difficult to accomplish, especially at the secondary level where a special education teacher might have different subject assignments from one year/semester to the next, or multiple subjects to handle in a single assignment. Given the current "highly qualified (HQ)" requirements of NCLB, one might expect to see more co-teaching and inclusive practices, especially at the secondary level. However, there are still places (separate schools, hospitals, and the like) where this would be impossible or very unlikely.

CEC has established standards around 10 domains. At each level of development (initial preparation, induction, and continual professional growth) teachers are expected to have different levels of expertise about each standard, but each standard is considered essential for good practice. They are included in Appendix A. Over 40 states are committed to aligning their licensing processes with the CEC standards. CEC standards are also aligned with the standards of the Interstate Teacher Assessment and Support Consortium (InTASC) and the National Board of Professional Teaching Standards (NBPTS), which give special educators a single set of guidelines and goals for practice.

CEC also commented on issues states face regarding teacher preparation and licensure (2009). Over the history of special education teacher licensure and certification, we have grappled with the dilemma of broad preparation versus categorical preparation. CEC notes that broadly prepared teachers might not be adequately prepared for the complex challenges they might face in their classrooms. On the other hand, narrowly prepared teachers might not be prepared for the diversity of students they meet. CEC expressed concern over teacher certification practices that rely too heavily, or in some cases exclusively, on a single test taken by the teacher candidate. NCLB currently includes a provision that a highly qualified teacher could be one who passes a single test, even though logically this does not seem like a high standard, given the complexities of teaching. At this point there seems to be no available test for adequately assessing the content and pedagogy required to be a truly "highly qualified" special education teacher.

Preparing Special Education Personnel

As stated in *No Dream Denied* (National Commission on Teaching and America's Future, 2003), teacher preparation must begin with what is known about good teaching. Therefore, in special education, we look to the standards set by the CEC, last revised in 2009. As noted in the previous section, CEC has set minimum expectations for teachers in the areas of standards-based curriculum content, individualized pedagogical content, and subject matter content. Furthermore, there are standards for the preparation of special education personnel. States, universities, and various accrediting bodies use these standards to shape preparation practices, as well as to evaluate teachers. The standards for the preparation of personnel from CEC are briefly noted below, and are contained in Appendix B.

1. A strong conceptual framework on the part of the preparing institution.
2. Candidates have mastered the appropriate CEC content standards.
3. Candidates have a solid grounding in liberal education (reading, written and oral communications, calculation, problem solving, thinking).
4. Candidates have an understanding of the general curriculum, teaching or collaborative teaching of the curriculum, and designing appropriate accommodations and modifications.
5. Candidates who will be assuming sole responsibility for providing academic content have appropriate content knowledge.
6. Programs have an assessment system in place.
7. Programs have appropriate field experiences available for candidates.
8. Programs provide experience with diverse populations of students.
9. Program faculty are well qualified.
10. The program has appropriate leadership, authority, budget, facilities, and resources.

CEC considers a well-prepared special education teacher to be one who has met the 10 content standards (see Appendix A). In addition to these 10 standards, there are also more specific standards for teachers of specific groups of students, as well as standards for paraprofessionals, and leadership standards. The standards provide important guidance for teacher education professionals; however, they lack specificity. This is both good news and bad news. The standards need to be operationalized at the local level, and brought into alignment with other considerations such as the conceptual framework of the preparing entity, local cultural context, area, and level of preparation.

ASSOCIATION OF TEACHER EDUCATORS

Another set of standards useful for special education teacher educators is from the Association of Teacher Educators (ATE, 2007). These are broad goals which have applicability for all teacher education programs. The nine standards for teacher educators are included in full in Appendix C. Briefly, they state that teacher educators:

1. Model good teaching.
2. Apply cultural competencies and promote social justice.
3. Engage in scholarship.
4. Are committed to professional development.
5. Provide leadership in program development.
6. Collaborate.
7. Advocate for high-quality education.
8. Contribute to improvement of teacher education.
9. Contribute to visions for teaching, learning, and teacher education.

The first standard, teaching, includes an emphasis on modeling. "In order for teacher educators to impact the profession, they must successfully model appropriate behaviors in order for those behaviors to be observed, adjusted, replicated, internalized, and applied appropriately to learners of all levels and styles" (ATE, 2007). The standard basically states that good teacher educators are good teachers. However, it goes further in stating that good teacher educators also have to make what they are doing explicit for candidates. It is not enough to "do" the good teaching practice, they need to say to candidates "this is what I am doing, and why I am doing it." It is good practice, then, for special education teacher educators to self-talk about teaching decisions and model self-regulation. The four types of self-regulation—self-monitoring, goal setting, self-evaluation, and self-reinforcement—should be modeled and taught to candidates just as we want them to model and teach them to their students.

Take, for example, a professor teaching a course to special education candidates with a doctoral candidate assisting in the teaching. The faculty member may explicitly model self-monitoring activities around their teaching practices (preparing a syllabus, keeping notes, preparing lectures, maintaining gradebooks) for the benefit of the doctoral candidate. She may also model goal setting by sharing with the doctoral candidate goals she has for teaching the class. She may model self-evaluation by reflecting with the doctoral candidate about teaching practices. Finally, the faculty member may model self-reinforcement by celebrating with the doctoral candidate at the end of the semester!

Standard 2, cultural competence, is also important to consider. Candidates first need to know their own cultures, which means that teacher educators do as well. As teacher educators, we should hold high expectations for all candidates, understanding their developmental levels, backgrounds, and so forth. Teacher educators need to help candidates to understand these concepts and to apply them successfully in their classrooms. Like Standard 1, teacher educators need to make these explicit and transparent in their own practice.

Standards 3 and 4 are related to aspects of a faculty member's job that are not directly related to candidate development. However, without engaging in scholarship and improving their own practice, teacher educators will not be adequately prepared to address candidates' needs. Standard 5, program development, is an ongoing process for most full-time special education teacher educators. In special education, changes in types of licenses granted to candidates or response to changing standards for K–12 students may necessitate change in programs. Also, as faculty shift in their own interest and expertise, different programs may be developed.

Standard 6, collaboration, refers to work with various stakeholders in teacher education. In special education teacher education, our stakeholders vary, but at least include our candidates, fellow faculty members (in special education and general education), public schools, parents, and the public in general. Collaboration is addressed in more detail in this book and is a major consideration in our practice.

The final three standards, public advocacy, teacher education progression, and vision, ask the teacher educator to look beyond the walls of an individual university and work toward improving experiences for all stakeholders, including ourselves. Special education has a rich history of public advocacy, and as special education teacher educators, we should continue to work toward improving outcomes for all.

LOOKING FORWARD

In conclusion, in order to have successful beginning special education teachers, preparation matters. Brownell and colleagues conducted a review of successful beginning special education teachers in 2005 and reached several conclusions. First, they noted that candidates need to be grounded in content, and while their particular review focused on reading instruction, there are additional content areas that candidates might be expected to cover, which adds to the complexity of a special education teacher's job. Greer and Meyen (2009) noted that typically candidates are relatively underprepared to teach mathematics in their preparation programs, whereas they are still expected to provide math instruction to their students. Indeed, anything at all that is taught in schools could be the responsibility of a special education teacher to address in some way. This might lead to candidates who are prepared in a shallow way across a great deal of content, or who might be prepared in depth in just a few areas of content. In the first situation, the candidate might not feel truly comfortable with any area. In the second, candidates might find themselves teaching in a content area in which they have little or no preparation.

One way to address this issue is to encourage or require dual licensure in special education and another area. However, this approach requires even more in the way of coursework and field placements and can be a barrier to attracting enough candidates. There is also a danger in a dual program of doing neither general education nor special education well, watering both down so that teachers leave these programs unprepared to deliver high-quality instruction to anyone.

The second finding (Brownell et al., 2005) was that successful beginning special education teachers are experts in classroom management. This is probably the area of most concern to candidates, schools, cooperating teachers, parents, and the general public. Special education candidates likely take the most coursework and get the most practice in this area, yet still typically encounter difficulties in the field. This is partly because of the nature of the students they encounter, but may also be due to the disconnectedness between what is taught in the university classroom and what the candidates experience in their field placements. For example, universities may teach candidates about positive behavior interventions and supports (PBIS), and local schools may also be moving toward PBIS models, be at various stages of implementation, and what the candidates experience might be very different from how they were instructed. The resulting cognitive dissonance can be disturbing to new teachers, and they may be more likely to adopt the practices of the schools in which they work, and disregard, discount, or have little chance to apply the education they received about best practices.

The third finding regarding successful beginning special education teachers follows naturally from the second. Candidates need a variety of high-quality practice sites, preferably where there is a close match to the philosophies and practices of the university, a close working relationship between the university and supporting school districts, and close supervision by the university (Brownell et al., 2005). Chapter 3 will address field placements in more detail.

Ethics

Fiedler and Van Haren (2009) called for focused attention on ethical principles in the practice of teaching. They pointed out that ethical dilemmas do exist in our field and advocated for professionals to know their ethical codes. The CEC Code of Ethics (see Appendix D) should be known by special education teacher candidates, and candidates and teachers need to be able to defend positions they take in their practice based on these codes. In their study, Fiedler and Van Haren found that 46% of their respondents, which included administrators and teachers in Wisconsin, had minimal or no knowledge of the CEC Code of Ethics. They noted that teachers have a more direct impact on quality of education, but that administrators are more often in the position of engaging in advocacy. They argued that professionals need to be able to articulate these basic ethical principles (which can be found in the CEC Code of Ethics) when confronted with an ethical dilemma: (1) beneficence and responsible caring, (2) integrity in professional relationships, (3) responsibility to community and society, (4) benefit maximization, and (5) equal respect (Fiedler & Van Haren, 2009, p. 162). This indicates that special education teacher educators need to be familiar with the CEC Code of Ethics, and how it relates to other ethical codes candidates and faculty may need to attend to. Teaching specifically about ethical issues and helping candidates to address ethical dilemmas should be carefully and intentionally infused into courses and programs.

Returning to Thiagarajan et al. (1974), addressing how teacher educators can prepare special educators, the stated objective was "to assist the reader in the design, development, and dissemination of instructional materials for training teachers of exceptional children" (p. 1). While some of the issues and procedures are outdated, there are many aspects that still hold true and are useful today when considering educating future special education teachers. Their statement that "as in other fields of teacher training, special education is undergoing significant changes" (p. 3) still holds true today. They presented a model of instructional development they referred to as the "Four-D Model," dividing instructional development into definition, design, development, and dissemination. In this book, I hope to address these issues in light of what we have learned in the intervening 35 years, while still remaining true to the original goal of enhancing preparation of special education teachers.

CHAPTER 2

Who Are the Candidates?

> It isn't a matter of money. It isn't a matter on the part of the army of desire. It's a matter of production and capability of doing it. As you know you go to war with the army you have—not the army you might want or wish to have at a later time. You can have all the armor in the world on a tank and it can (still) be blown up. . . .
> —FORMER U.S. SECRETARY OF DEFENSE DONALD RUMSFELD (December 2004)

Just as Secretary Rumsfeld pointed out that we have "the army we have," suggesting that it is no use wishing for a different group of soldiers, in teacher education, we have "the candidates we have." Of course, he was criticized for this position—after all, giving volunteer soldiers needed armor, and spending money in recruitment and preparation, could indeed assist them in being more effective at their jobs. Likewise, while we have the volunteer candidates that we have, giving them more tools to use and better preparation can help them to be more effective. To do this effectively, we need to have at least some understanding of who the candidates are likely to be. Also, understanding our potential candidates can help us encourage them to give special education serious consideration.

This chapter will briefly discuss what we are discovering about learning and the brain as it relates to knowledge of our candidates and their students. Next, in light of the information explosion and the rapid pace of changes in technology, how can we assist our candidates in acquiring needed knowledge? How do we recruit candidates who will be a good "fit" for the profession? Finally, the chapter will describe and discuss two groups of candidates we are most likely to encounter—millennial students and career changers.

BRAIN PLASTICITY

It used to be common knowledge that the brain becomes "fully formed" early in life and that many things are unchangeable after a certain point. Worse, after a certain point, decline in brain power was seen as inevitable. We now know that the brain is constantly changing, based on what parts of the brain are used and not used. Indeed, lifelong learning is possible and a reality for many, as long as we continue to actively learn. "Cells that fire together, wire together" is a common adage. For example, people may associate smoking cigarettes with certain activities, making quitting smoking difficult if one still wants to participate in those activities. Likewise, learning certain tunes can help us remember other things—hence, the alphabet song is put to music so that children can remember the order of letters. Now we know that our brains are shaped by experience; it is not as "hardwired" as we once assumed. This should give us hope! As special educators, haven't we always operated under the premise that humans have the capacity for enormous changes in learning and behavior? Now, current brain research is backing up that belief.

Just as the brain is always capable of change, and we are capable of learning new skills, we are also capable of forgetting those things we do not practice. Continual learning is essential in mastering something—"If you don't use it, you lose it," in other words. Current external forces on brains today, especially those of younger people, include the realities of scarcity, fragmentation, and an emphasis on competition and winning (Marshall, 2005). Marshall argued that the current nature and unnatural design of education leads to shallow, rather than deep, learning. This leads to learners who are risk averse, unengaged, and ill equipped to deal with complexity. That is certainly one possible outcome of the combination of the information explosion and the high-stakes environment of U.S. public schools. However, if teacher educators and other leaders in the field can work to transform educational practices, we might be able to effect positive change for schools.

The idea of "brain plasticity" is one commonly explored in popular media as well. A recent Google search on the term yielded 886,000 results, with 84 news results (July 2, 2010). Advertisements for "exercising your brain" abound. The troubling part of this explosion of information is that it is difficult for many people to separate the "real science" from the "snake oil salesmen." Teacher educators, including myself, typically do not have deep knowledge in the area of neuroplasticity, though it is in our best interest to learn as much as we can, especially as it relates to special education. At the same time, we must remain skeptical of revelations that seem too good to be true and assist our candidates in making these distinctions as well.

One of the common themes from the "brain change" literature concerns how the youth of today have such vastly different brains from those of older generations due to their consistent exposure to electronic communication. While this may be true, it is also true that each generation is faced with different challenges and opportunities. Availability of different technology through the years has likely always changed our brains, just as practice or lack of practice with different tasks has changed our brains. The difference is that we now have the capability of investigating what those changes look like. I am not sure that the changes are positive or negative, but they are certainly adaptive. What we must do, as teacher educators, is recognize that we are teaching candidates who are different from us in these ways, and that they will be teaching students who are different from themselves, and from us.

PREDICTING THE FUTURE

I took my first course in technology for educators in 1982, as a graduate student at San José State University. We were taught the needed skills of splicing 16mm film, laminating, and creating overheads. At one course meeting, we were brought into a computer lab filled with Apple computers. We were just there to look at them, not to use them in any way! At that point in teacher education, I am sure that my professors, even in the newly burgeoning Silicon Valley, could not conceive of my need for computers on a daily basis, nor could I imagine it myself. Even further from our minds was the likelihood of my nonverbal students being able to communicate using various technologies, or that students (and teachers) could communicate instantaneously with other students and teachers across the world.

How much more rapidly is the world changing now, in the early part of the 21st century? We are preparing candidates for a job that we cannot imagine—nor can they. What do we need to know in order to do this? Candidates, to survive, must learn to be critical consumers of research, and of potential interventions. Beck and Kosnik (2006) suggested that candidates need to be able to evaluate what is important, and invent appropriate practices. Instead of having to "invent" appropriate practices, while sometimes necessary, it is more valuable, as suggested elsewhere in this book, that candidates be able to evaluate appropriate practices in light of their knowledge of teaching, learning, and their students and situation.

The key to understanding our candidates, as well as the students they will teach, is the key to being successful in almost any endeavor: FLEXIBILITY. Encouraging our candidates to have an open, curious, and flexible attitude about their careers and their students will assist them in becoming successful teachers.

As teacher educators, we should have the same open, curious, and flexible attitude about our careers, which will assist us in becoming successful teacher educators. Beck and Kosnik (2006) addressed the question of how to teach for an unknown future. They suggested that teacher education programs should foster inquiry. As they said, the ability to study a situation, and notice what their students care about, is more valuable than particular approaches. As we teach our candidates to appropriately respond to students' individual needs, we likewise need to respond to the individual needs of our candidates. Many of us were educated before the Internet, email, podcasting, and so on were even possibilities. Today's candidates are not only up to date on these technologies, they use them and expect us to use them. In fact, as I was writing this paragraph, two of my graduate students contacted me via Facebook chat from their internship site in Tanzania! In the "class of 2014" report from Beloit College, we discover that this class views email as archaic and too slow (*www.beloit.edu/mindset/2014.php*).

Guiding and Being Guided by Candidates

In our preparation programs in the early part of the 21st century, there is little patience for the old practice of "chalk and talk." Simultaneously, what we know about education has progressed. Our candidates are right: we need to teach things that are relevant, have applicability sooner rather than later, and provide connections to their lives. One issue that arises with learners in the 21st century is that knowledge of how to use the technology in their daily life does not mean that they know how to appropriately use these technologies for teaching and learning, or know about and understand the variety of technology that their students may use for their own learning (such as adaptive technology). Therefore, we have to be familiar with the technology used by candidates, and how they use it. Then, we need to guide them in the process of using that information, and the schema they already have developed, and apply this to their pedagogical practice.

Candidates today may intimidate some teacher educators with their familiarity with current technology. At the same time, we probably still have to explain conventions of writing, concepts of reliable sources, plagiarism, and so forth. Candidates may view a professional journal online and a blog entry online and see them as having equivalent trustworthiness. Teacher candidates may be more versatile and comfortable with technology, but they still need guidance to use technology as professionals. It is our job as teacher educators to help candidates think about the technology they take for granted as a possible tool for their own education or the education of their students, and to introduce them to alternative ways of accomplishing their goals. As we find ourselves moving into 21st-century ways of learning, knowing, and teaching, we move away from our own familiar, comfortable teaching practices (Berry, Norton, & Byrd, 2007). In this way we will find better ways of preparing prospective teachers.

RECRUITMENT

Encouraging candidates to enter any field is tricky. What do we need to know about them in order to help them make good decisions and have the best candidates possible in special education? The field of special education is largely unknown to those outside the larger field of education, and is misunderstood by many within education. How can we best explain to potential candidates about the field of special education and the variety of roles that special educators take? By the same token, what do we need to understand about our potential candidates?

In their discussion of the potential candidates currently enrolled in college, Hardman and West (2003) addressed why they might choose special education as a field of study. These "gen X" and "millennials," like previous generations, may see special education as a higher calling. They foresee that they can and will make a difference. This generation has been recognized as having the quality of being committed to organizations that are committed to them. These traits are similar to the mindset of many professionals, including current faculty in universities. Hardman and West suggested beginning to socialize prospective doctoral students to the higher education culture early—as early as in undergraduate study. This gives those of us in initial preparation programs dual tasks: preparing special education teachers and preparing future colleagues. This is an important consideration for teacher education programs that don't have doctoral study, because as candidates leave their initial preparation programs and eventually enroll in doctoral work, if you maintain a relationship, they may be interested in returning to your university for a job.

One current way candidates are recruited into our programs is by universities' alignment with and participation in alternative routes to teacher preparation. Regardless of the explosion of alternative routes to teaching, the vast majority of candidates receive at least some of their preparation in universities. So-called alternative routes typically involve at least some interaction of candidates with universities. New special education teachers who are in these alternative routes come from one of several sources. They include those who have not been in a traditional teacher preparation program, either cross-categorical or category specific. They may be teachers who have general education training, and are taking courses or other forms of professional development to become certified. Some candidates seeking alternative certification may be pursuing a second career. Some may take courses that are district designed, in which case the preparation may be for generic teaching, not for specialized content or a specialty area of special education. Some of these candidates may also have no educational training, and yet are working in the schools as teachers while pursuing licensure. This latter group has the most catching up to do, as they lack both content and teaching skills.

Educating candidates who are not licensed, but are teaching, raises contradictory dilemmas of quality and quantity (Sindelar & Rosenberg, 2000). As we find

Counseling against a Career in Special Education

From time to time, special education teacher educators may find themselves in the difficult position of needing to meet with a student and suggest that they choose a career outside of special education, or even outside of education altogether. In fact, if a candidate shouldn't be in special education, then probably general education is no better a match, since general education teachers need to meet the needs of special education students also.

This is a difficult position for a number of reasons. First of all, the shortage of special education professionals is probably of concern. If someone is willing to enter the profession, why keep them out? Secondly, pressures from universities to increase enrollment, particularly in programs that tend to have lower enrollments (like special education), might make it seem like the university faculty member is working against his or her own best interests. Finally, as special educators at heart, it is in our nature to believe that anyone can learn nearly anything that is learnable. To "give up" on a student seems to be equivalent to admitting defeat.

Regardless, as special education teacher educators, we may have a candidate who, despite our efforts in providing an excellent education, is not successful. Some situations are straightforward: the candidate cannot pass our courses, the candidate breaks the law so that they are not allowed in schools, or the candidate violates a university regulation (e.g., plagiarism). At times, though, the candidate is not exhibiting needed knowledge, skills, or dispositions that we want in future special educators, and yet they are passing our classes, allowed in schools, and not going against university regulations. What can a teacher educator do in this case?

If the faculty member has a good relationship with the student and feels that a conversation might be helpful, that might be all that is needed. If not, one strategy is to bring other people in on the conversation, especially if the conversation might be difficult. A department chair, dean, or fellow faculty member can help to corroborate the concepts that you are trying to convey. Someone from the university's learning support center might be a good resource as well. In most cases, you are not the only one who has had these same concerns. (If it is just a single faculty member with concerns, a great deal of self-reflection is probably in order before drastic steps are taken with the candidate.)

This is not a move to be made lightly, and it is important to help the candidate "prove you wrong." Be as specific as possible in what you have noticed about the candidate, and provide as much evidence as is available. Be prepared with options for the candidate—other career paths that may use the candidate's strengths better than special education. Be as positive and nurturing as possible—especially if the candidate might be surprised by your assessment.

In the end, the candidate might remain in your program. If so, it is important to reassure the candidate that you are not "out to get her." If you are the candidate's advisor and other advisors are available, offer to let the candidate switch. If you feel strongly about the candidate's fitness to be a special educator, and the candidate remains in your program, it is necessary to keep good documentation of all discussions, observations, and so on. For example, after a face-to-face or phone conversation, it is wise to follow up with an email to the student (and perhaps the academic advisor, department chair, or other parties) with a summary of the conversation. That provides documentation of the meeting, as well as a chance for clarification. Keep in mind the most important outcome of all is providing excellent educators for the schools!

ourselves walking this tightrope we are faced with very real external demands: legislative mandates for curriculum coverage, restrictive institutional rules and regulations, and candidates' growing consumer orientation. However, separating traditional preparation from alternative routes may be a false dichotomy. Doing so also implies that all alternative routes are comparable. It may be true that the candidates have different requirements, but universities may be able to provide some advice and influence in establishing what is needed for the "bare bones" of teacher preparation. In my own experience teaching in public universities in North Carolina, in any given class I might have candidates who are seeking their first special education degree (with or without another education degree), an advanced special education degree, or an initial license not tied to a degree—or are simply taking the class to further their own professional skills. Furthermore, candidates may have years of experience in the public schools as teachers, teacher assistants, or other professions, or they may have no teaching experience whatsoever. It is important as special education teacher educators to understand the needs of each of these groups of students, and, as good special educators, address the needs of each student while maintaining standards of academic rigor and professional behavior.

WHO ARE THE STUDENTS?

> It has always been the practice of those who are desirous to believe themselves made venerable by length of time to censure the new comers into life, for want of respect to gray hairs and sage experience, for heady confidence in their own understandings, for hasty conclusions upon partial views, for disregard of counsels which their fathers and grandfathers are ready to afford them, and a rebellious impatience of that subordination to which youth is condemned by nature, as necessary to its security from evils into which it would be otherwise precipitated by the rashness of passion and the blindness of ignorance.
> —SAMUEL JOHNSON (September 8, 1750)

As the quote from Samuel Johnson reminds us, and as stated previously, the concept of a "generation gap" is nothing new. As teacher educators, we are always in the position of preparing candidates for a future we cannot foresee, just as they are preparing their students for a future they cannot foresee. We teach our candidates about the structure of public education, and of special education, and about who their students are, as well as what best practices are for teaching those students. As we are doing this, we realize we are merely describing the present, and that all these structures and practices may change in the future. It is important for us, as special education teacher educators, to have the most up-to-date information available to us and our students, encourage our candidates to be inquisitive, lifelong learners, and arm them with a basic set of skills and competencies which will serve them well.

In describing the current generation gap, Hardman and West (2003) wrote that many tensions are due to profound economic changes we have seen and are seeing, such as periods of plenty followed by near Depression-era joblessness. Recent generations were raised in a culture of immediacy. They think and communicate in the information age. They are used to a lot of information available all the time. Their parents were likely divorced, and/or both work, so they were more likely to be "latchkey" kids. One interpretation of their behavior is a short attention span, perhaps based on a need for immediate information and feedback. These candidates have a profound need to be independent and face problems on their own. In choosing affiliation with a profession or organization, Hardman and West suggested that there are four questions these potential candidates have: Can I belong here? Do I have access to information? Will I be able to work independently? Will I know if I'm successful? To be successful special education teacher educators, we need to be prepared to address these questions and provide truthful, satisfactory answers.

Millennial Students

One group of candidates we are likely to meet, partially described in the previous paragraphs, have been dubbed "millennial students," entering the universities in the early part of the 21st century hoping to become special education teachers. This generation includes those born between 1981 and 1999 who grew up with very different experiences from those of us who did not always experience "information overload." Some of the characteristics of these millennial students have been described in several places (Hardman & West, 2003; Kirkwood & Price, 2005; Korir Bore, 2008; Mabe, 2007; Monaco & Martin, 2007; Oblinger & Oblinger, 2005) and include:

Plugged In

Millennial students have continual access to the world around them via a multitude of electronic means. Besides radio and TV, there is the Internet, cell phones, iPods, GPS systems, cameras, and so forth. If a candidate has a question about something, they are as likely to use a search engine such as Google, or ask the question of their Facebook friends, as they are to ask someone in their environment (professor, colleague) or go to the library to look at a book or journal. Admittedly, many of us who are not part of this generation may use the same techniques, but the difference is that today's candidates find these techniques to be second nature, and the obvious first (or only) step in acquiring information. As teacher educators, we need to insert ourselves in these technologies and use them—maintaining a blog or a Facebook page; using Skype, Google chat, or other available technology. As we use these tools ourselves, we have more credibility with our candidates as we educate them about how to make judgments about the quality and veracity of information found on the Internet and other such sources.

Use of web-based instruction to prepare special education teachers (and others) is becoming increasingly common. In a study of web-based preparation of special education teachers, Korir Bore (2008) found that while many students appreciated the convenience and felt they had sufficient interaction, others missed instructor presence. What was found to make a difference in quality was the instructors' technology skills and knowledge about web-based instruction. Just as "one size fits all" is not appropriate for students, it is inappropriate for candidates.

Don't Read Newspapers/Books

Since needed information is available (accurate or not) via more immediate means, candidates today are less likely to turn to a book. Newspapers are folding or combining or shrinking in the current environment, as we are depending more on online sources for news. In the future, the look of newspapers and books could change drastically, and indeed is already changing. One can purchase a variety of "readers," such as Kindle, or an iPad. While books themselves are unlikely to disappear altogether, it is probably reasonable to assume that information about special education, teaching, and students will more likely be found in a more immediate, or at least in an electronic, environment. It is important for teacher educators to become familiar with the technology our candidates use so that we can assist them in using these resources wisely.

Impatient

Since information is immediately retrievable, there is little patience for waiting to get it. This spills over into other areas as well; candidates may be less likely to put forth the effort required to acquire teaching skills, or have the patience to allow their students time to learn. Candidates need to realize that to be an expert in anything takes time, effort, and guidance. With the availability of "fast-track" and "on-the-job" preparation, it is reasonable that some individuals may see special education as an easy job. While it might be an easy job to obtain, it is a much more difficult job to keep, and to do well.

Goal Oriented

Candidates today are much more goal oriented than previous generations. This is good news for us as they may be more likely to persist toward their goals, and will hold us accountable for helping them make adequate progress. We need to pay attention, therefore, to what candidates and graduates of our programs tell us regarding the success of our efforts. (More information about assessing our efforts is in Chapter 6.) They have also been described as pressured—they are used to being judged and expect it. Candidates raised in the latter part of the 20th century were brought up to believe they could achieve great things, and while they will work toward these great things, they may not be prepared for failure to reach goals.

Learn by Doing

Candidates today are more interested in learning by active involvement than by listening to lectures or reading books. This has some very specific implications for special education teacher educators. Candidates will learn better, and deeper, by role playing, simulations, and field experiences. Field experiences (as expanded on in Chapter 5) have long been critical to the education of teachers. Therefore, we might assume that millennial students will be successful, and willing to participate in the wide range of field experiences that are recommended. Those involved in team-oriented experiences, common in special education, also will be likely to succeed. These students are accustomed to working in groups, and contributing.

Used to Instant Feedback and Feel They Deserve It

In our plugged-in society, candidates are accustomed to receiving feedback quickly. Waiting for scores, critiques, and final grades seems unnecessary to people who can find out so much information instantaneously. Therefore, special education teacher educators are under increased pressure to provide quick feedback, and to explain why some feedback may take longer to provide. We often need to give candidates thoughtful feedback which will lead to deeper learning. If we can intersperse assignments that require that type of feedback with assignments where we provide more instantaneous feedback, we may be able to strike a balance. Use of peer feedback and other cooperative assignments can also give students interim feedback on their work.

Have Friends from Different Cultures

Candidates today are more likely to have grown up around much more diversity than candidates in the past. In 1990, the percentage of the Anglo population in colleges was 79.6. It is predicted to reach 57.6% by 2050. All of the net increase in the college population is expected to be accounted for by minority students (Murdock & Hoque, 1999). Today's candidates are therefore likely to have friends who don't share the same first language, or even friends living anywhere in the world whom they only know virtually. This should increase the probability that they are more tolerant and understanding of differences, and understand various cultural differences which influence their students' approaches and attitudes to learning. Trent, Kea, and Oh (2008) reviewed research on the incorporation of multicultural education into both general and special education programs. They noted that inexperience on the part of university faculty might partially explain why multicultural education is not more fully integrated into programs. Given that our candidates may be more experienced than teacher educators, we can leverage their strengths to help us gain understanding.

Need Flexibility

We can point to several pieces of evidence which indicate that our candidates need flexibility. First of all, the continuing proliferation of alternative routes to licensure is indicative of this need. Secondly, candidates are more likely to seek out online learning for all or part of their teacher training. They are less likely to be full-time university students (Kirkwood & Price, 2005). This means that special education teacher educators, to meet the needs of these realities, should look carefully at these new ways of instruction and ensure that they are of sufficient quality that candidates are still equipped to teach their students. Ultimately, this need of flexibility is to our advantage, as we seek to instill a flexible attitude toward learning and teaching in our candidates.

Don't Write Letters

Candidates are for the most part unfamiliar with personal letters sent via the postal service. They are more likely to text one another, or post something more publicly via electronic means. Even email is considered to be "too slow" for millennial students. This ties in with the expectation of immediacy and instant feedback. Candidates may need the skill of letter writing to communicate with some parents, though. Additionally, we may need to discuss with candidates the reasons professionals may want to give more thought and time for certain types of correspondence. Therefore, special education teacher educators may have to directly teach this skill, whereas their counterparts may not have had to in the past. In fact, the writing habits of these students does not necessarily translate to their abilities with all forms of writing, and as teacher educators we often find ourselves providing writing instruction to students which would have been considered prerequisite in previous generations.

Hate Busywork

This characteristic is problematic. Actually, any instruction or practice that candidates cannot see an immediate application for may be labeled by them as "busywork." When a special education teacher educator has spent a great deal of time carefully crafting an assignment or course of study, and the feedback is that it is busywork, the special education teacher educator needs to look at it and ask two questions: Is the assignment actually necessary and adding to the capabilities of the candidate to teach? Has the assignment been explained adequately enough to the candidates so that they understand the purposes and desired outcomes of the assignment? While some assignments and courses may accurately be labeled busywork, it is as likely that the issue is one of miscommunication between the teacher educator and the candidate.

Career Changers

Another population of candidates we encounter in special education teacher education is career changers. These candidates may be changing to special education for a variety of reasons. They may have lost their jobs due to a poor economy, they may be returning to school after raising a family, or they may have children of their own with special needs which spurs an interest in the field. With these varied backgrounds, it is difficult to describe what these candidates are like. Dickar (2005) conducted a study of career changers in comparison to recent college graduates and reached several conclusions.

Most obviously career changers may have a need to catch up to their younger peers at times, especially regarding technology. However, willingness to use technology is not always a generational issue (Oblinger & Oblinger, 2005). Many times in teacher education programs, instructors will have some candidates who are career changers and some who are traditional college-age candidates. Teaching a diverse group like this, with a wide variety of backgrounds, prior knowledge, and expectations, can be a challenge. Special education teacher educators and entire programs may be inclined to focus on one group or another. However, special education teacher educators should keep in mind the principles of universal design in their own instruction. For example, grouping students heterogeneously for projects can be one way to achieve our goals.

Like traditionally prepared teachers, some career changers perform below expectations and some exceed expectations (Dickar, 2005). Those performing below expectations in Dickar's study were found to have only a casual interest in teaching and were just interested in employment. They tended not to get along with their students, and had difficulty with the flexibility needed to adjust to school culture. In contrast, traditional-age teacher candidates who performed below expectations seemed to be insecure with their authority, and could be described as "playing at" being a teacher. Career changers who exceeded expectations had a strong motivation to teach, exhibited strong professional behaviors, and were able to synthesize newly learned theories and skills and put them into practice.

Miller, Brownell, and Smith (1999) conducted a study investigating what led to candidates staying, leaving, or transferring from their teaching jobs. They discovered that four factors contributed to candidates staying in their jobs: current certification, perceived stress, school climate, and age. For those who left or transferred, there was no significant difference among these factors except current certification, with teachers inappropriately certified being more likely to leave. Special education teacher educators are in a position to influence all of these factors (except age). We are therefore in the business of providing not only appropriate skills, but a path toward appropriate certification. The more skills and training we provide the more we can help address stress. Addressing issues of school climate with candidates and how they can contribute to a positive school climate can give candidates a feeling of control of their own destiny in schools and their career.

CONCLUSION

As has always been the case, all teacher candidates have personal needs which need to be addressed to help them be successful. These include support from peers and faculty, and teaching and interacting with a non-authoritarian attitude. A social constructivist view of teaching and learning is a useful way of thinking about our instruction. This view contains the belief that knowledge is socially constructed, and that learning is an interactive process that occurs between and among all participants. While several models and frameworks for education are available, many teacher education programs have adopted this approach (Beck & Kosnik, 2006). This approach models an integrated approach to life and learning, including connecting all aspects of life, and promoting a caring and supportive teacher–student relationship. In a social constructivist model, knowledge is social and experience based. All aspects of a person are considered to be connected. For special education, this fits with our understanding of learning as well, especially the idea that learning communities should be inclusive and equitable. If we operate out of such a framework in our teacher education practice, supporting candidates in addressing their personal needs will be second nature. Still, there is a balance to strike between supporting candidates in this way and maintaining consistent standards for candidates in our programs.

> We're the middle children of history . . . no purpose or place.
> We have no Great War, no Great Depression. Our great war
> is a spiritual war. Our great depression is our lives.
> —From the movie *Fight Club*, referring to Generation X

I do not intend this chapter to be interpreted as "Kids these days. . . . " Each generation can, and has, remarked on the differences between their generation and the ones that follow. We may see our candidates as having negative qualities, or positive qualities. Very likely, like all of us, they have both. At the same time, these changes between generations do represent a real shift. As special education teacher educators, we need to assure that candidates understand what we understand about the field, about students, about learning. We must be flexible not only in our delivery of content and pedagogy to our candidates, but also in how they deliver instruction to their students. Candidates who are already practicing teachers (such as some master's students) may experience a lot of cognitive dissonance. As special education teacher educators we have to help them work within their small world of school or district (or state department of instruction), while at the same time giving them a larger "worldview," or at least a national view, of education.

> Since we can't know what knowledge will be most needed in the future, it is senseless to try to teach it in advance. Instead, we should try to turn out people who love learning so much and learn so well that they will be able to learn whatever needs to be learned.
> —JOHN HOLT

CHAPTER 3

Field Experiences

A "Must Have"

You can observe a lot by watching.
—YOGI BERRA

We learn by example and by direct experience because
there are real limits to the adequacy of verbal instruction.
—MALCOLM GLADWELL, *Blink: The Power of Thinking*
Without Thinking (2005)

Field experiences are among the most important components in the professional
development of quality teachers. As is the case with a variety of other human service professions (e.g., medicine, social work, counseling), supervised field experiences provide appropriately trained candidates with opportunities to apply freshly
acquired skills within nurturing and supportive environments.... Field experiences
bring emotion and immediacy to the teacher-education process. With a built-in net-
work of supervision, developing teachers are (a) placed in real-world situations, ...
(b) given ample opportunities to improve on their assessed deficiencies, and (c)
encouraged to enhance creatively their areas of strength. (Rosenberg, O'Shea, &
O'Shea, 2006, pp. 2–3)

Virtually all teacher education programs require field experiences—they have
for quite some time, in fact. In special education teacher preparation, this is no
less important. As candidates may be responsible for multiple grades, multiple
setting types, and so on, well-planned and multiple field experiences are critical.
Brownell and colleagues (2003) found that effective teacher preparation programs

tended to emphasize one to two practicum experiences and a semester or year-long student teaching placement. Depending on what areas of licensure are being sought, even this amount may be inadequate. The reality of the breadth of experiences needed further emphasizes the need for collaboration between universities and K–12 school settings.

There is abundant evidence that field experience is the most important part of a candidate's education. In a 2001 article on supporting beginning teachers, Whitaker noted the need to adequately prepare candidates for their first year of teaching with practical experiences and real-life problem solving, and revise curriculum in response to candidate/completer difficulties. Once candidates have completed their programs and graduated and/or received licensure, they must be competent in a variety of areas on the first day of their first job. Therefore, the higher quality and the wider variety of field experiences that can be provided to candidates, the more likely candidates will be successful.

Beck and Kosnik (2006) suggest that practica be interspersed throughout the program. Darling-Hammond (2006) noted the need for well-defined standards of practice and performance which are used to guide and evaluate coursework and clinical work. She also noted the need for extended clinical experiences which are carefully developed to support the ideas and practices presented in simultaneous interwoven coursework. In the best cases, special education teacher educators will be able to make a careful selection of mentor teachers and provide professional development for mentors, encouraging their participation in meetings, seminars, and assignments, therefore better linking campus and "the field."

This chapter includes suggestions about how to do this effectively as well as how to "work around" potentially challenging scenarios. First, I discuss why field experiences are important, and several issues teacher educators face in finding good field placements. Next, I consider the features of good field experiences. The literature in general education as well as special education has much to say about field experiences and how they should be developed, designed, and executed. In special education, as in other fields, finding a quality field placement for teacher candidates can be challenging, so I also address how we might use field experiences to influence what is happening in the field. Finally, I address the development of teacher educators in supervisory roles.

WHY FIELD EXPERIENCES ARE IMPORTANT

Billingsley (2005) recommended that principals hire special education teachers who have completed a "strong preparation program with extensive field requirements" (p. 46). In order to facilitate this quality in their potential hires, these principals bear responsibility for providing some of those field placements for teacher candidates. Principals and university faculty can work together to match cooperating teachers with candidates and their preparation program. This can be accomplished by teacher educators creating and strengthening relationships with practicing teachers and principals, as well as other administrators. As special education teacher educators, we have valuable information to share with practicing teachers, and being available for professional development serves multiple purposes for our own professional development as well. As university faculty, we are expected to be fulfilling the roles of teaching, research, and service. By working with public school partners, we may be providing service to public schools (service), cultivating potential partners for research (research), and cultivating good field placements for our candidates (teaching).

This statement speaks to the importance of field experiences for candidates. Experienced special education teacher educators have heard candidates say many times "I didn't learn anything until I got to student teaching." Of course, without adequate preparation before student teaching, they might not have benefited from even the best placement. Statements like these may sound like indictments of the coursework of teacher preparation, but might be more accurately heard as "Once I got to student teaching, the education I had received up till that point really gelled for me and began to make sense." The process of learning any skill, including teaching, is not complete without practice. As Zeichner, Melnick, and Gomez (1996) pointed out, the best we can ever do in preservice education is to prepare candidates to begin teaching. A critical part of this education, according to Zeichner and colleagues, is to prepare candidates to take control of their continuing education.

Relationship between Teacher Preparation and Field Experiences

Billingsley (2001) reported several areas of good news regarding special education teacher preparation and field experience. She found that 75% of beginning teachers stated that their preparation program matched the realities of their first school assignment. She also found that beginning teachers who were fully certified for their teaching assignments had student taught for an average of 15 weeks, whereas those who were not fully certified had an average of 11 weeks of field experience prior to their first job. The particular route to certification (bachelor's degree, advanced study, alternate route, and others) was not reported along with these data, though the various entry paths of the beginning teachers were given elsewhere in the report (46% bachelor's, 31% master's, 10% alternative, 7% continuing education, 5% fifth-year program).

No matter the length of placement, it is of course the quality of those placements and the supervision offered which makes the difference. Billingsley (2001) also reported that 65% of beginning special education teachers reported that they had a formal mentoring program in their first job, which is a substantial improvement over the report of 28% of experienced special education teachers who said mentoring was available for them when they began teaching. However, special

Teaching about Local Practices

Candidates, especially those who already work in local schools, may express a preference for learning details about local practices. A common place where this happens is in coursework where they are learning about IEP procedures. Their reasons for wanting to learn "the forms" stem in part from their observations of teachers who refer to the IEP process as merely filling out paperwork. In this case, they see understanding the underlying reasons and general good practices as an unnecessary waste of their time. On the other hand, they may also need to understand how those general practices fit into their own practices with those particular forms. So, should we as special education teacher educators teach specifically about local practices? Like all answers regarding teaching practices, the correct answer is "It depends." It depends on the goals of the particular class and instructor, the understanding of the candidates, and the usefulness of the local forms.

Probably the major reason for not using the local forms to teach about practice is that the forms themselves may not represent best practice. Most local school systems nowadays have adopted good IEP practices, but it is possible that the forms themselves might be too vague to use in a college classroom and may require more specific staff development within the context of the school system.

Pedagogically, it may not be best practice to use local forms since it may prevent candidates from seeing the "big picture." If the focus is on "filling out paperwork," candidates may not understand that the IEP forms are an outcome of a multidisciplinary team meeting, focused on addressing the needs of a particular student. Another reason not to use the forms in teaching is that candidates may overgeneralize from a local example. IEP forms and other paperwork vary from LEA to LEA, and even subtle differences may confuse some candidates and new teachers.

On the other hand, using local forms may help candidates feel more at ease with the process. In states where each district uses essentially the same form, these are often available on the SEA (or LEA) website, and using those materials (and sometimes training guides) can assist candidates to ease into their first jobs with one less thing to worry about. Having already looked at the forms, and having a greater opportunity to discuss and ask questions about them in a college classroom, will help them understand more about local practice.

The recommendation here is to use a blended approach. A general guide to writing IEPs (such as Bateman & Herr, 2006) should be used as a major text, but assignments and examples could come from the use of local forms. This will help candidates make the connection between best practice in the profession and best practice in the local situation.

education teacher educators cannot rely on a candidate's first job experience to provide education that should have and could have come during their training program. We should consider their preservice experiences carefully, and provide scaffolding so that they can benefit from first-year mentoring experiences.

In the best-case scenario, there is a seamless connection from coursework to fieldwork to actual practice. However, there are many potential pitfalls along the way. The fieldwork connection is one of the most important for addressing the tension between coursework and actual practice. The effective field supervisor plays a critical role for the candidate, but also for the university and the school district, and can play an important part in connecting research and practice. Supervision of fieldwork experiences is addressed in more detail later in this chapter.

FINDING GOOD FIELD PLACEMENTS

In any critique of teacher preparation, and of special education teacher preparation specifically, the importance of quality field experiences is emphasized. Programs need to be in the business of connecting theory and practice, and help candidates learn to analyze teaching (Darling-Hammond & Baratz-Snowden, 2005). Supervised practica are critical, and as candidates develop a wide repertoire of teaching skills, it is part of the field supervisor's role to help them integrate this knowledge and eventually to become adaptive experts. While taking classes in pedagogy, content, and theory are important to developing good special educators, candidates must have the opportunity to practice these skills in a supervised setting, receive feedback from professionals and others, and come to feel more confident in their practice. While this is a given in teacher education, finding quality field placements can sometimes be an elusive goal. Some of the issues include:

1. Special education classrooms may not be staffed with fully certified, experienced teachers. Universities typically have guidelines for how teacher candidates are placed into particular classrooms and student teaching experiences. These include at a minimum that the cooperating teachers be appropriately certified for their position. Other factors that may be required by the institution, receiving school district, or special education program include completing a certain number of years of teaching, holding an advanced degree, having a certain number of years in the current setting, or more. In special education, this can be difficult to achieve as there are generally fewer special education teachers to choose from, compared to, for example, the number of available elementary education teachers. When preparation programs are categorical, this is further complicated. If exceptions to these policies need to be made, then it is incumbent on special education faculty to defend such decisions, keeping the professional preparation of our candidates at the forefront of consideration.

2. Special education classrooms might not be providing "best practice," or practice that aligns with the goals and objectives of the training program. For example, the university may emphasize the importance and value of inclusive education, but the school or school district may educate students separately, or have students in inclusive settings that do not represent best practice. The university is then in a dilemma of choosing a good teacher in a separate setting or searching further for a better match. Given the constraints already described, the "better match" may not be possible. It can be expected that candidates will do better with a cooperating teacher who provides high-quality instruction regardless of circumstances. If the preparation program has done a good job advancing their perspective, and the field supervisor can help the candidate with the cognitive dissonance resulting from being placed in a less-than-optimal setting, the overarching goals of the candidate and the program can be reached.

3. Candidates may already be working as paraprofessionals, and there may be precedence or practice to let them shift to a student teacher/apprentice role within that same classroom. However, if that particular setting isn't a good placement from the university's perspective, this can be difficult to negotiate. Even if the university had identified the particular school and classroom as a good placement choice, allowing a paraprofessional who is also a candidate to be placed there in another role would not expand the candidate's horizons, nor necessarily increase his or her skills. There is also the danger of the candidate merely continuing in the role as paraeducator, and therefore not getting the full student teaching or practicum experience. A variety of field experiences broadens candidates' experience, and more placements across a training program is better. One approach to this dilemma would be to have a cohort of candidates who could trade or shift positions for their field experiences. This would keep the same number of personnel in the classroom, while broadening the candidates' experiences, thus making them more valuable to future employers. Coordinating this among field placement offices, cooperating teachers, candidates, and school districts can be complex, but will pay off in the long run as these relationships are established. Typically, school districts are interested in working something out, as the candidates would likely seek employment in that district as a special education teacher upon program completion.

4. There may not be room within a training program, due to other requirements, for more than one or two field placements. Candidates may be seeking licensure to work in a variety of settings, with a variety of disability labels, or in a variety of age/grade placements, but may still finish their training unprepared for what they encounter as teachers. Special education teacher educators need to do their best to provide a wide variety of experiences for candidates, so that they can make informed decisions about what job or jobs they might want to do upon completion of the program. When actual practice is not possible or available (see paragraph 2 above), technology allows candidates to observe and interact via

video, two-way TV, computer simulations, and so forth (e.g., Grossman, 2005; Knapczyk, Hew, Frey, & Wall-Marencik, 2005).

5. When candidates are already practicing teachers, working with an emergency license of some type, quality field experiences may be impossible. In these cases, it is important to provide opportunities for them to observe other programs, either in person or virtually, and have time and opportunity to reflect on these observations in a meaningful way. We could require these candidates to compare other programs to their own practice, and to best practices indicated by available literature or other areas of focus. If these observations are required as part of coursework assignments, reflections can be tied to the particular topic being addressed. Typically, observation of other programs requires time away from jobs, but if schools are interested in increasing the skills of their teachers, it would be in their best interest to facilitate observation of other programs.

6. Field supervision is often relegated to individuals who are not truly connected with the special education faculty (Meyen, 2007). Adjuncts and graduate students often fill this role, and in fact this may be a good use of these individuals' talents. Some adjunct instructors, however, may not share the goals of the program or be knowledgeable about them. They may have their own agendas and ideas about teacher preparation. It is important that special education teacher educators communicate with field supervisors as well as cooperating teachers and candidates to address this issue as thoroughly as possible. To that end, and to strengthen the classroom–field connection, I offer two suggestions: First, adjuncts and graduate students who serve as field supervisors need to be involved and included in curriculum discussions of the special education faculty. Second, the "regular" special education faculty should be involved in field supervision on a regular basis. Even if they (we) just do it once a year, for just a minimum number of students, it can help us stay grounded in what is happening in the local schools. The longer special education teacher education faculty stay in the field, the further they are from actual teaching experience. For example, my last year as a public school teacher was 1992–1993—since then IDEIA has been reauthorized twice (including the addition of two disability categories), and NCLB and other accountability measures have taken education in directions unforeseen 20 years ago.

FEATURES OF GOOD FIELD EXPERIENCES

In addition to formal practicum and student teaching, experiences in the field can be offered candidates through well-crafted assignments during coursework. These activities can be seen as part of scaffolding teacher preparation skills for candidates. While they might not allow for a full teaching experience, they do provide opportunities for practice and to receive feedback on discreet skills.

Such activities could involve tutoring individual students, practicing administering assessments, or practicing teaching discreet lessons or units. Candidates might also be given assignments to interview principals, parents, students, and others involved in special education. Simulations are another way to help candidates practice skills. In one program, for example, faculty in a college of education formed "IEP teams" for candidates to practice running IEP meetings (Werts, Mamlin, & Pogoloff, 2002).

Role of Supervisors

The main goal of field experience is to provide good, meaningful practice for candidates. Teacher education programs, in general, need to connect theory with practice and help candidates learn to analyze teaching. In order to do this, attention needs to be paid to providing supervised practica. This assists candidates in developing a wide repertoire of teaching strategies, and should help candidates become adaptive experts (Darling-Hammond & Baratz-Snowden, 2005). In special education, becoming an adaptive expert is even more important to our practice. Supervisors of field experience, then, have a role as mentors in this process, as do cooperating teachers. In Table 3.1 I have suggested common placement activities and assignments for candidates in field placements. Along the way, having candidates reflect on their experiences will not only assist them in their growth, but assist the field supervisor and cooperating teacher in knowing how to assist the candidate.

CEC addressed the development of new teachers and established guidelines as to what a mentor looks like (CEC, 2009). The guidelines stated that new special education teachers become proficient more quickly with the support of veteran

TABLE 3.1. Placement Activities and Assignments.

- Defining goals for the placement—either individually or in consultation with the IHE, LEA.
- Variety of placement activities.
- Acclimation to the environment.
- Observation.
- Tutoring individuals/small groups.
- Gradual taking on of responsibilities.
- Practice developing classroom management skills.
- Full-time, supervised practice teaching.
- Planning field trips, schoolwide activities.
- Include practice in collaboration, IEP team leadership, assessment.
- Participation in the whole school (faculty meetings, field trips, PTO meetings, noninstructional duties).

Note. Where appropriate, include meaningful, guided reflection on part of candidate.

special education teachers. They also recommend an intensive and focused induc-tion program wherein the mentor is in the same or similar role. The mentoring guidelines can also be considered when aligning student teachers with cooperat-ing teachers and university supervisors.

Loughran and Berry (2005) noted several practices related to modeling. They suggested unpacking teaching practices through professional critiques and high-lighting different types of teaching decisions to inform novice teachers about pedagogical reasoning. This indicates that as teacher educators we should engage in explicit modeling of our teaching practices, incorporating "think-alouds" as we teach our candidates. Loughran and Berry also suggested highlighting the distinction between action and intent, the difference between what one intends to teach and actual teaching. Again, this can be made explicit for candidates.

At times, supervisors may find themselves either distant from their candi-dates or in need of more frequent contact. One potential model was developed by Knapczyk and colleagues(2005). They described online mentoring for limited-license teachers in the area of behavior disorders. In Indiana, a limited license is a temporary teaching permit for an individual who holds a bachelor's degree, but not an education degree in the appropriate field. These may be called "emer-gency" or "temporary" in other places. Each limited-license teacher had one or two mentors, posted weekly progress reports on their activities, and engaged in online dialog with mentors. The mentors' role was to give ongoing guidance and consultation. This allowed for a high-quality experience for candidates and supervisors, even though they were scattered geographically.

Choosing Good Placements

Darling-Hammond (2006) offered suggestions for constructing the clinical expe-rience, including learning to look in classrooms, assuming graduated respon-sibility, and preparing clinical placements. This included the development of school and university partnerships. She suggested a lab school or professional development school (PDS) model. Similar approaches are problematic in the area of special education in the 21st century. In a typical school, there are likely to be too few special education teachers to support enough candidates to make a dif-ference in the supply of special education teachers. Special education candidates from a single program are typically placed in multiple schools, and even mul-tiple school districts. A lab school could only host as many candidates as they have special education teachers. On the other hand, a lab school experience does give candidates an excellent opportunity to see the convergence of coursework and practice in an explicit way. If there are lab schools or PDSs available, special education teachers may use them during coursework for observation, or specific class assignments. They could therefore benefit from the modeling of the teachers in the setting, even if they do not have opportunity for more extensive fieldwork there. Another way to think about PDS models is to partner with several schools or an entire school district, using principles similar to the single-school model (D. Cooper, personal communication, October 10, 2010). This has the benefit of university faculty having a wider influence on practices (as discussed below).

Grossman (2005), in her review of pedagogical approaches in teacher education, argued that microteaching and lab experiences were based on atheoretical research, with a focus on what works and not why. This is important when conducting research, but, in a practical sense, if these approaches are deemed successful for candidates and their students, then *why* they work is less important. Microteaching and lab experiences can give candidates exposure to discreet teaching skills, which will eventually need to be put together in a culminating lab experience (student teaching, or something similar).

All of the issues thus far noted apply regardless of the type of preparation programs candidates are enrolled in. Since alternative routes are not usually a formal part of a university program, there is more flexibility, which is a double-edged sword, as it means there is more risk to a candidate in preparation. Bergeron and colleagues (2005) gave the conditions for success for candidates prepared in alternative routes. These included communication, use of cohorts, field experiences, partnerships, practical experiences, and use of technology, which are similar to the conditions needed for traditional candidates.

Teaching Candidates to Observe

Darling-Hammond (2006) wrote about an "apprenticeship of observation," which would include university faculty modeling teaching, and modeling teacher thinking. But how do we teach our candidates to be good observers? Part of the answer, as suggested earlier, is to explicitly model for candidates and provide supported practice in observation. Provenzo and Blanton (2006) provided extensive guidelines for helping students observe in schools and draw conclusions about what they are observing. Their text is not limited to special education candidates, but the observation instruments and guidelines could easily be used as is, or adapted or modified for particular purposes.

Helping Candidates Transition to "New Teacher"

The transition from candidate to student teacher to beginning teacher can be stressful and overwhelming in the best circumstances. As teacher educators, we can assist in this transition in several ways. One idea is to bring first-year teachers back to the university to speak to candidates about their experiences (Whitaker, 2001). This can not only assist the candidates, but be a support to the first-year teachers as well. Another thing teacher educators can do is encourage graduates to seek support and follow-up during the first year, including offering graduate courses on mentoring. Lava, Recchia, and Giovacco-Johnson (2004) wrote that first-year teachers need to know about the complexities of their multiple roles, including knowing how to deal with children, adults, and administrators. They also must come to terms with their expectations versus the reality of their job. They must be able to handle a range of needs, various curriculum trends, lack of resources, lack of recognition, and unrealistic expectations. These myriad demands can be lessened in practica settings by providing transitional support.

One issue to consider is the fact that many new teachers will not remain in their jobs. Billingsley (2005) reviewed the research and provided several reasons special educators might leave their jobs, including personal reasons, first-year teacher problems, multiple and interacting work problems, isolation and lack of support, role problems, stress and burnout, and lack of preparation. In terms of lack of preparation, she noted that special education teachers may be hired for positions for which they are not certified. For example, an individual may be certified to teach students with learning disabilities, but be hired to teach students with autism.

Another common experience many new teachers have is the diverse makeup of their caseloads. It is likely that new teachers will have greater diversity in terms of disability labels in their classrooms than their preparation or licensure would suggest appropriate. A SPeNSE report (Westat, 2000) found that 80% of special education teachers have students with two or more primary disabilities, and 32% reported having four or more primary disabilities represented on their caseloads. Another issue is the difference in cultural and linguistic diversity among students between candidates' student teaching placement and their first teaching position. Nearly 25% of special education teachers' students are from cultural or linguistic groups different from the teacher's, and 7% of their students are English language learners (ELLs). The SPeNSE report stated that teachers need to be innovative, adaptive, and prepared for a wide variety of students, tasks, settings, and situations. This report has implications for the whole of special education teacher preparation, but is especially pertinent when considering field placements.

Using Field Placements to Influence the Field

In the best-case scenario, the goals of the public schools, special education teachers in those schools, teacher candidates, special education teacher educators, and universities mesh in a productive way that leads to growth for everyone involved. However, there are more typically roadblocks along the way. For example, teacher preparation programs may emphasize direct explicit multisensory instruction as best practice, while the available placements may use more holistic or discovery learning. Or, schools may proclaim to be using inclusive practices, but are still using poor teaching practices regardless of where the teaching is occurring (Mamlin, 1995, 1999).

How can special education teacher educators place candidates in less-than-optimal settings and through the placement of the candidate shape the practices in that setting? One way is through various assignments that might be given to the candidates to complete in the setting. For example, candidates may be required to complete a teaching unit using self-regulated strategies instruction, including data collection and decision making. In this way, the candidate with the guidance of the field supervisor hopefully models best practice for the cooperating teacher. In these cases, it is best that the field supervisor be an expert in the practices being taught, and he or she needs to be involved in the situation enough to ensure that the candidate is performing the skills well.

Another way special education teacher education programs can help influence practice is by offering cooperating teachers faculty development at the university or at another site. Examples include providing courses in being a cooperating teacher, providing tuition waivers for cooperating teachers' own personal development, and day-long (or more) workshops for cooperating teachers' to take advantage of at the university or in the school district. A nice incentive for cooperating teachers would be for universities to provide substitute pay to offset the cost of the cooperating teacher's absence to attend professional development. Teachers who agree to become cooperating teachers typically do so out of some larger concern for the field and desire for professional growth and may welcome information from either the university supervisor or the special education program in general to help improve their own practice.

Conversely, school systems can provide up-to-date information for universities. For example, they may be well under way in implementation of an RTI process while university faculty are just becoming familiar with it. In this case, the school system is in the position of providing professional development for the university faculty, keeping special education teacher education up to date on how policies are being operationalized in the field. School system personnel may also serve as guest speakers, co-teachers, or adjuncts for the universities, strengthening the school–university partnership. Candidates often appreciate learning from professionals who are "in the trenches." All of these activities can also help increase the movement of "research-to-practice."

> What we have to learn to do we learn by doing.
> —ARISTOTLE

Development of Teacher Educators in Supervisory Roles

Ritter (2007) reported on his own progress as a new teacher educator. In this self-study, he noted that as he began his practice as a teacher educator, he identified more with the teachers, and didn't seem to have the "long view"; his initial feedback to candidates (student teachers) was prescriptive and he positioned himself as an expert. As he continued, he became more of a co-learner with the student teacher, and was able to engage in collaborative reflection. This is similar to the progression that all of us make as we travel from novice to expert in any field. School systems often have programs in place to help with the transition from candidate to teacher. Universities may or may not have mentoring programs, which may or may not involve mentoring around being a teacher educator.

As teacher educators, as in many fields, it becomes important to identify one's own mentors and to serve as mentors when appropriate. Ritter's (2007) self-study focused on several tensions inherent in teaching teachers, which he labeled as (1) telling versus growth, (2) confidence versus uncertainty, (3) safety versus challenge, (4) planning versus responsive, (5) valuing versus reconstructing experience, and (6) action versus intent. Identifying these dilemmas in our own practice as special education teacher educators, and seeking resolutions, we can continue to provide meaningful growth and opportunities for candidates.

In conclusion, it is difficult to imagine a teacher preparation program that does not require an internship or student teaching experience. Universities have various constraints and requirements for what should occur in these experiences. Since special education candidates are typically preparing to teach a wide variety of students in a wide variety of situations, special education programs should seek to provide as much practice in authentic settings as possible, perhaps surpassing the minimum requirements of the teacher education program in general. This role, mentoring the next generation of special educators, is one of the most important we have.

CHAPTER 4

The "Job" of a Special Education Teacher

Nothing is particularly hard if you divide it into small jobs.
—HENRY FORD (1863–1947)

It's not a 9–5 job. It's an every moment you're awake job
because you actually enjoy the work that you're doing.
—JEFFREY KALMIKOFF, *Designing for Community
with Zero-Advertising Brands* (2006)

Imagine this scenario: You're at a party and meet someone new. In the course of conversation, you discover that she is an electrician. "Oh," you say, "an electrician! How interesting! You know, I have grown up around electricity all my life and you know what I think ought to be done about lighting someone's house? I think that everything should be done so that lights come on just by thinking that you want them on. And the wire that you use these days is so wasteful! You need to use this new kind of wire I read about on the Internet that is made out of recycled egg cartons and titanium. That's what I think!"

Well, of course this is absurd and the electrician would be well within her rights to let you know how ridiculous your statements are. You are ill informed, and your assertions seem to be based on hearsay and weak evidence (if any). Why, then, is the scenario acceptable if the profession in question is education? This chapter will discuss what special education teacher educators can do to assist candidates in becoming acclimated to the profession of special education and how to assist them in continuing to strengthen the profession.

Perhaps the first question to answer is whether or not teaching in general, or special education in particular, is a profession. Many jobs we consider professions now were not always considered so, and had to "earn their way" to professional status. Consider the profession of dentistry. This was not always considered a profession. From 7000 BCE, there has been evidence of dental practices, including the first bridge in 700 BCE. However, dedicated dentists didn't exist until the 16th century. Prior to that, the work was done by doctors and barbers. The first dental school was founded in Maryland in 1840, nearly 9,000 years after humankind started working on the problems of healthy teeth (*dentalassistant. net/pictorial-history*)! Nowadays, of course, there are few if any individuals who would willingly go to a dentist who had not gone to dental school but had only expressed an interest in dentistry, and within the first year of practice attempted to take and pass the licensing exam. Moreover, the public in general would not consider those dentists to be "highly qualified" based on those few actions.

IS SPECIAL EDUCATION TEACHING A PROFESSION?

Most people, if asked, would say that teaching is a profession. However, as raised by Connelly and Rosenberg (2003), teaching may not fully fall into that category. I have been told that the difference between a job and a career is that "you can go home from a job." In special education, and in special education teacher education, in fact, the "homework" is never ending. In this regard, one often overlooked but very important skill we can pass on to our candidates is the skill of taking time off. Clearly, some candidates who come to us as undergraduate (and some graduate) students don't need role models for taking time off! However, most special educators (and teachers in general) are dedicated to their jobs, and in many school cultures it is considered appropriate and desirable to take work home for evenings, weekends, and summers. This may be fine in the short term, and work well for even the first several years of one's induction into the field. However, at some point, there needs to be some time to rejuvenate, for both mental and physical reasons.

Connelly and Rosenberg (2003) addressed the issue of special education's professional status in a COPPSE report, comparing teaching to the fields of medicine, engineering, law, and social work, and their various routes to attaining professional status. They concluded that at this point education could be classified as a semiprofession, based on its movement toward meeting the traditional standards of a profession: (1) degree and complexity of knowledge required, (2) length of induction period, (3) continued professional development expectations, (4) specialization and expertise held by members, (5) amount of authority over one's actions, and (6) relatively higher salaries. In general, to be considered a professional, a special education teacher must be competent, knowledgeable, and effective. Special education, they assert, in its current state is similar to where professions such as law, medicine, and engineering found themselves as they were developing, and is similar in more ways to social work and its current standing on the professional continuum.

Connelly and Rosenberg (2003) concluded with several questions which they asserted need to be resolved to move special education more firmly toward professional status. These include questions surrounding licensure, course of study, value of professional preparation, the role of government as well as market-driven considerations, and who monitors and controls the supply and demand of personnel. They concluded that teacher education and teaching need to take action on these points. While these are important issues, which continue to be discussed and reshaped, most in the field of special education write as if the field has already achieved professional status.

Likewise, this chapter (and the entire book), is written as if special education, and to a certain extent special education teacher education, has already achieved the status of a profession. In the following pages I use Connelly and Rosenberg's (2003) characteristics of professions, and what we as special education teacher educators need to pass on to teacher candidates to assist them in becoming members of our profession. I will also, when possible, address how special education teacher educators may contribute to increasing special education's professional status.

Degree and Complexity of Knowledge Required

Teaching is a complex endeavor. Special educators need to understand various student conditions, the general school curriculum, pertinent laws, and specialized pedagogy. In many ways, special educators have played and always will play the role of being "everything to everyone." The special educators in schools are the people to turn to when there is anything unusual about a student, or if a student is experiencing academic difficulty. Special educators are assumed to have a depth and breadth of knowledge, or at least knowledge about how to acquire the needed information. This makes the special education teacher educators' job an enormous one. With luck, the special education teacher educator is working in an environment where there are other professionals with expertise to draw on, just as it is fortunate when the special education teacher is working with other professionals who have some of the required knowledge.

However, like the special educator, the special education teacher educator may also be working in an isolated situation. It may be that there is not more than one person with expertise in a particular category, even if there is more than one special education faculty member. So, the lone special education faculty member is in a position of making sure all candidates have the breadth and depth of knowledge to perform their complex tasks upon entering the field. Chapter 5 addresses the areas of knowledge that are needed; the point here is that since so much knowledge is needed special education might rightfully be considered a profession.

Lengthy Period of Induction

In the best of circumstances, there are a variety of internships with seasoned professionals before special educators enter the field. However, the field still struggles with the need for more agreement on what is adequate and the expectation that all special educators will enter the field only after this period of induction. More research is needed to determine what an adequate minimum induction period should be. This is one area where much more work is needed to help special education move toward actual professional status. It is possible, for example, to enter a special education (or other) teaching job, with all the rights and responsibilities that entails, after producing proof of an undergraduate education in any field, and perhaps passing a single exam. If it is possible for someone with no supervised field experience to enter the teaching profession with the same responsibilities as someone who has gone through a rigorous teacher training program, be paid the same salary, and be given the same level of employee supervision, then we are a long way from being considered a profession.

As special education teacher educators, there are several things we can do. First, we can work to provide larger numbers of teacher candidates who have gone through a rigorous program. Second, we can work cooperatively with school districts and other entities that provide quicker routes to licensure to help ensure that the "fast-track" candidates/teachers are receiving as much supervision as necessary. As noted over 15 years ago, and still true today, educators can be part of the profession after a 4-year degree, rather than follow more prolonged entry into the field such as happens in law or medicine, both of which require advanced degrees and prolonged apprenticeships (Cruickshank, 1996). In recent years, the number and types of "fast tracks" to entering the profession have increased, compounding this issue.

Expectation of Continued Professional Development

To retain their teaching certification, in most cases teachers must demonstrate that they have continued learning in some way, either through advanced coursework, attendance at workshops, or attendance at district-sponsored faculty development opportunities. This varies by state, however. As disheartened as we might feel with the issues surrounding lengthy induction to the profession, one thing that special education (and education in general) does have in its favor is the expectation of continuing education. There are multiple opportunities for continued professional development, from very brief workshops which might be held as part of a faculty meeting at a school, to day-long districtwide workshops, to state, regional, and national workshops, meetings, and conventions. Another way for teachers to continue their professional growth is to seek advanced degrees, or take coursework to lead to licensure in other areas.

The key to making sure these activities help move the field toward professional status is professional development that is meaningful to the teacher or the candidate. The activities might not be exclusively in the area of special education. Professional development in technology, reading, mental health issues, social skills, and other areas would be meaningful to all educators. Special educators, as they work more closely with general educators, and with the general education curriculum, may need to avail themselves of more professional development in content areas. In middle and high schools, special educators may be responsible for multiple content areas, which may change from year to year (or semester to semester), so they will need to look for professional development in those areas.

Expertise and Specialization in the Area

Special education teachers have specialized knowledge which sets them apart from other educators and other professionals in schools. There is also opportunity within special education for further specialization. In several states, the first teaching license that a candidate is eligible for is a generic special education license, allowing the novice teacher to teach across grade levels, disability areas, settings, and so on (*www.tqsource.org*). This helps schools and school districts fill positions as teachers are more flexibly licensed, and novice teachers can "try out" several different teaching scenarios. However, it puts enormous pressure on special education teacher educators to provide broad-enough knowledge to candidates. We can help candidates find their niche by providing them with enough information and field experiences to help them make an informed decision about where to take their first job.

In any case, this does represent specialized knowledge. With a broad special education teaching license, can these teachers still be considered to have specialized knowledge? Yes. The skills and knowledge of a special education teacher are different from the skills and knowledge of general educators. The competencies developed by CEC (see Appendix A) provide the framework for many programs that educate special education teachers more generically. As special education teacher educators, even if we are working in a categorical program, we need to attend to these competencies since our candidates will very likely encounter students with a variety of disabilities as they enter the field.

Additional specialized knowledge often comes after the novice teacher has some experience in the field. Whether or not the areas listed on the license itself change, teachers may decide after some experience that they need or desire additional expertise in a particular area of special education, whether that is a categorical area such as traumatic brain injury, or autism, or perhaps is a pedagogical area such as strategies instruction, applied behavior analysis, or inclusion.

One thing that sets education apart from other endeavors, or special education apart from other fields of education, is the same thing that sets any field of study apart from another. There is a commonly accepted body of knowledge, ways to approach new information, and basic standards, which are largely known to "insiders" or members of the profession, but remain unknown to the general public. As noted above, the field of education has experienced issues related to its establishment as a "true" profession. This occurs for a number of reasons. Cruikshank, as early as 1996, suggested, for example, that one obstacle to teachers having true professional status includes a lack of consensus among educators regarding what constitutes the required specialized body of knowledge and skills for effective teaching.

This lack of consensus is still descriptive of what is going on in teacher education in general, and special education teacher education in particular, in this early part of the 21st century. There is disagreement among special educators at all levels: Should special education teachers be pedagogical experts? Should they be content experts? Should they be experts primarily in social and behavioral issues? General education also has a variety of opinions about what they want and need special education to be: Should special educators be experts at helping students pass high-stakes tests? Should they be available to help teachers have some students removed from their classes? Should they work side-by-side with general educators on the general education curriculum? Should they just be responsible for the parts of the curriculum that general educators do not cover (such as functional skills)?

Retaining Authority over One's Own Actions

Authority, the next attribute of a profession, is more problematic, though special education teachers often have more authority than some other teachers may have. Special education teachers may exert influence via their leadership on IEP teams, and often have more autonomy than other teachers may have in choosing methods of instruction. Some of the difficulty arises in that as special education teachers we are in a service profession, and often are public employees. We are, as special education teacher educators, essentially training individuals to work in public schools. In order for this aspect of the job to be in place so that special education is considered a profession, special education teachers, and teacher educators, will need to win over the trust of the public who employs them, so that authority can be granted to general and special education teachers. As special education teacher educators, helping our candidates to do their job well, with confidence, and with good leadership skills, we can assist the special education in moving toward becoming a bona fide profession.

Relatively Higher Salaries

Obviously one area where special education teachers are no different from other teachers in schools, and teachers in general, is teacher salaries. Special education and other teachers are not well paid compared to other professions. However, as mentioned above, they usually work for the public, and thus are remunerated based on the local tax structure, at least in the United States. (There are other countries that do provide teachers relatively high salaries and associated benefits.) In general, the public considers teachers to be among the most important individuals in their communities, and in many cases might be appalled that they are so underpaid.

In fact, special education teacher educators, especially in the beginning of their careers, may be teaching candidates who are drawing a higher salary than they are, if they are new assistant professors teaching experienced teachers. Taking into account the time off from earning to complete graduate studies, it would not be unusual for university faculty to never "catch up" in lifetime earnings. Clearly for both educators in K–12 schools and teacher educators in universities, there is more than salary driving our desire to be a part of the profession. On the other hand, if the public were to put their money where they say their trust is, higher salaries would certainly not be refused!

It is also logical that the shortage of teachers and the lack of monetary reward for teaching contribute to the feeling that teaching is not a true profession. At this point in our history, at least in the United States, it is difficult to foresee either of these obstacles being removed. The persistent teacher shortage, especially in special education, leads to an emergency situation and the general public cannot wait around for teachers to gain more experience before entering the field. In law and medicine, if there are not enough professionals, individuals who need their services merely have to be put on a waiting list for the next available opening. We do not have that luxury when it comes to students in schools.

SUPPLY AND DEMAND

Historically, special educators have been in great demand relative to their supply. Sindelar, Brownell, and Billingsley (2010) noted that the demand for special education teachers has hovered at around 10% for decades. They also noted that the literature has suggested that extensive preparation might mitigate attrition, which is another historic problem with supply and demand. While alternative-route programs might produce a greater number of competent teachers, they suggested that more extensive programs might be more cost effective due to lower attrition. They also noted an impact on attrition from the availability of new teacher mentoring.

One of the issues of supply and demand is that while federal policy has tightened and increased standards on teacher quality, they have at the same time encouraged ways to ease entry into the profession (Sindelar et al., 2010). The requirements of NCLB (now ESEA) has helped to deprofessionalize entry into special education teaching, since teachers who are enrolled in alternative or fast-track programs, passed a test, or majored in a content area can be given highly qualified (HQ) status without further preparation in special education, disability studies, or pedagogy. Funding for teacher education is another ongoing issue. Kleinhammer-Tramill, Tramill, and Brace (2010) reported that funds have been available for personnel preparation for special education teachers since 1958 but "funds have never been and will never be sufficient to supply continuing needs" (p. 195). Kleinhammer-Tramill and colleagues noted that the funds serve as "catalysts" to improve programs. They note that while dollars for personnel preparation have gradually increased from 1970 to 2004, the purchasing power of those dollars has remained flat, or slightly decreased.

There is an assumption (abroad and in the United States) that effective K–12 teachers will be effective teacher educators. This assumption is based on the implication that teaching experience is context free and thus transferable (Martinez, 2008). There is no evidence to support this nor any to refute it, either. However, there are specific things that teacher educators need to know about and be able to do. These include understanding adult learning in general, and understanding that teaching adults in noncompulsory settings requires a different set of strategies and skills. Likewise, teacher educators must be able to model and be explicit about the practice of teaching.

Another obstacle, as suggested in the opening scenario, might be that education is one profession that most people have had some prolonged interaction with as they were growing up. There is, then, the perception that it is relatively straightforward to understand everything about education because the vast majority of people have experienced it. Therefore, it has become difficult for education to achieve true professional status because it is apparently understood by the general public. Indeed, the public exerts much control over both public and private education in every aspect from financial control to laws governing education. The public, especially in the case of public schools, "owns" the educational enterprise. There has been criticism *about* this, including contrasts with other professions which are monitored and regulated by members of that profession (e.g., medicine, law, and plumbing). Until educational associations are able to exert more direct influence on the job of teachers, this is likely to continue to be an issue.

TEACHER EDUCATION'S ROLE IN ADVANCING THE PROFESSION

Careful reflection on one's own experience can certainly help candidates as they begin to learn about the field of education, but they need to understand that they enter the field with an incomplete and idiosyncratic view of education. It is our task as special education teacher educators to bring candidates into the profession of special education, and encourage them to view their jobs as special education teachers as a part of a larger, professional community. One way special education teacher educators can model this is by talking to candidates about professional organizations and how they assist the special education teacher educator to do their job. The CEC Code of Ethics (see Appendix D), for example, can be shared with candidates as a statement of the profession's philosophical and professional identity.

Cruickshank (1996) reminded us that professional courses are not intended to be of interest or value to those outside the profession. Therefore it can be challenging, at times, to shepherd needed courses through university curriculum committees. Arguments about why there should be "a graduate program in reading" or a "course on inclusion" may need to be taken on by special education teacher educators in an informative, respectful way so that the profession's identity can be maintained and furthered. The value of each person's profession is self-evident to them, but not necessarily to the larger community.

Cruickshank (1996) described 29 teacher education programs, which were all elementary or secondary preparation programs. In this report there was no mention of special education as a field of study or a mention of the need to know about special education for general educators. There was a brief mention of multicultural education. However, nearly a decade later, Pugach (2005) found in her research on preparing general education teachers to work with students with disabilities that 45 states and the District of Columbia required special education coursework for general education. So the field of teacher education in general does seem to be moving toward understanding the need to include special education in all training programs. Given the current requirements of ESEA and the increase in interest in inclusive practices in the schools, this is not a surprising development.

In university teacher preparation programs, typically one or more common courses are required of all teacher candidates. These include courses about foundations of education, perhaps an introduction to teaching course, sometimes a history and philosophy of education course. In most cases, very little is shared with candidates about special education's place in the overall picture of education, largely because the instructors in those courses typically have little experience with special education. The history of the field of special education, indeed, tends to get short shrift in most courses in special education as well.

In a study of commonly used special education texts, Mamlin (2009) found that while 20 of 28 evaluated texts addressed the history of special education in some fashion (sometimes with no more than a few sentences or a paragraph), only four spoke of the history of education in general. Most of these texts, in fact, only went back to 1975, or perhaps to the 1954 *Brown v. Board of Education* decision in describing the history of special education, but typically not much further. Giving candidates a sense of their place in the history of special education and where the field has come from will help instill a sense of professionalism among candidates. We have a need to educate our candidates about the history of the field, how we got to where we are now, and what current responsibilities are.

As teacher educators, we must consider how to go about teaching about local practices so that the information will be useful to prospective teachers. Sometimes these are excellent examples, sometimes not, but maintaining positive relationships with local schools is likely important! Also, we need to help our candidates make connections between what they learn in coursework and what they see in the field. Knowing major concepts is one thing, but on the ground applicability is useful as well.

Focus on diversity and inclusion is an important concept for teacher candidates (Brownell et al., 2003). These areas may be among those that teacher educators themselves have little first-hand knowledge of, and indeed many teacher candidates may have more information to offer here—these candidates, for the most part, have "grown up" with special education students in their classes and schools, whereas those of us who graduated prior to the mid-1970s likely had no experience with the education of students with special needs as peers in the classroom. On the other hand, special education teacher educators of a certain background may have experienced first hand the racial integration of schools and have much to share with candidates about those experiences. This is a case where sociocultural or constructivist concepts of teacher education (Beck & Kosnik, 2006) are useful and represent a good opportunity for the various generations to inform one another. In this arena, we, as teacher educators, have the overall information and knowledge about diversity and about inclusion. We have the theoretical basis and the research available to us. Our candidates have information about how these issues have played out in their own circumstances. Our job, then, is to help the candidates see how their experiences fit into the "big picture," and help them continue to move the profession forward.

ISSUES FACED BY CANDIDATES AND NOVICE SPECIAL EDUCATION TEACHERS

Teacher candidates have a range of background information about the job of a special education teacher. Some of them may have accurate information, while others may have outdated information, or little information. In many cases, the information candidates have is distinctive. There is a tendency for people, especially novices, to view their world as representing the entire universe, and it may be difficult for some candidates to accept that there are various approaches to educating students with disabilities, not just the one or two approaches they have encountered or heard about. A competent special education teacher educator will stay abreast of trends and practices in the field and be able to give the "broader view" to candidates.

Helping Candidates Make the Transformation to Professionals

Special education teacher educators have a role beyond merely providing needed coursework for candidates, especially when the candidates are part of an undergraduate or graduate degree program. To add to the professionalization of special education, we need to encourage our candidates to see their careers as those that reach beyond their own classroom or caseload assignments. There are several ways to approach this at a university. Perhaps the most obvious way is to sponsor or advise a chapter of the Student Council for Exceptional Children (SCEC). Local chapters are connected with the national organization, and can be provided with more experiences and resources in the way of professional development and connections with local service opportunities.

Another option, in addition to or instead of SCEC, is the inclusion of service learning opportunities to existing coursework. Some universities now require community service or service learning as part of degree programs, and special education teacher educators can help special education teacher candidates in individualizing their service to help them understand the profession better.

A final suggestion for candidates to explore is to either volunteer or work with the university's disability support center. These support centers may be in need of tutors who have some understanding of the individual needs of students, and who may have some understanding of how to assist students to study and learn strategically. Working with the disability support center can give candidates some real-world experience with students who may be in a better position to provide them with good, ongoing feedback than a student they might encounter in the local K–12 schools. If candidates do pursue this as an option, it will be important for either the special education teacher educators or the professional staff at the university's disability support center to help candidates understand the differences between the IDEIA and the Americans with Disabilities Act (ADA) of 1990 (ADA, 2009) so that they can provide appropriate support for the college students.

It is also useful, inasmuch as it is possible, to help candidates predict how changes might occur, at least in the near future. For these reasons, if for no other, special education teacher educators should stay involved in research, both as consumers and contributors. Attendance at state and national conferences by both special education teacher educators and candidates can help develop and maintain the "long view" that is desirable. It is important to give candidates a good grounding in these areas, and then to help them develop the attitude of flexibility and a lifelong learner. These attitudes are reflected in Standard 9, Professional and Ethical Practice, in CEC's professional standards for special educators (CEC, 2009):

> Special educators are guided by the profession's ethical and professional practice standards. Special educators practice in multiple roles and complex situations. . . .

Special educators engage in professional activities and participate in learning communities that benefit individuals with exceptional learning needs, their families, colleagues, and their own professional growth. Special educators view themselves as lifelong learners and regularly reflect on and adjust their practice. . . . Special educators actively plan and engage in activities that foster their professional growth and keep them current with evidence-based best practices. Special educators know their own limits of practice and practice within them. (p. 28)

There are, of course, multiple influences on the roles of a special educator, as there are with anyone working in the public arena. In special education, we must answer to local, state, and federal constituents. Primarily, for the special education teacher, concern is for the students and families included in his or her caseload. However, a good special education teacher educator will assist candidates in being aware of and informed about the influences on their jobs that come from beyond the classroom. With each new election, whether of a school board member or a U.S. president, new emphases and resources will influence the job. For example, as of 2011, ESEA is being considered for reauthorization and will likely modify some of the requirements of NCLB which altered practices in schools in the previous decade. CEC's current recommendations to the federal government regarding this reauthorization include some strong guidance for both special and general education, and if all these ideas are incorporated into the reauthorization, special and general education roles will change at all levels.

As teacher educators, we need to steer clear of "because I believe it" and look carefully at data as they become available to us. For example, inclusion may be conceptually/morally a great idea, but do the results indicate that this is the way to go for all students all the time? Under what conditions? If inclusion is a push of a preparation program, there is a need to focus on how to do it well, and how teachers can help effect change. Likewise, today candidates need to learn about PBIS and RTI, especially if either is a part of local practice. Besides just learning the local nuts and bolts of implementing these initiatives, though, candidates need to have some understanding of the issues surrounding it in the field at large. Even though inclusion, PBIS, and RTI may someday take a back seat or otherwise become "decided issues" in our field, the modeling of a critical approach to these ideas can assist candidates in taking a similar approach to ideas they will encounter in their careers. The point is that special education teacher educators should be able to disseminate to candidates what is currently known about particular practices, as well as about techniques for evaluating future practices they may encounter in their careers.

Candidates face several issues when learning to teach, and while making a transition to a beginning teacher. As teacher educators, we should be mindful of them, and address them in our work with candidates. Darling-Hammond and Baratz-Snowden (2005) divided these concerns into three categories:

misconceptions about the job, difficulties with enactment of skills, and dealing with complexity.

Misconceptions about the Job

Special education candidates enter the field for a variety of reasons. Special education is not usually an "obvious" job in the schools from students' perspectives, unless they received services themselves or had a sibling or close friend who received services. Some potential candidates may have had experience with special education while in high school through a tutoring program or teacher cadet program, so may have more of an idea of what special education is. Still others may have parents or other family members who work in the schools either as special educators or with special educators, so that information about special education as a profession is passed on through those connections. In all of these cases, though, the information that the potential candidate has about the job may be incomplete or idiosyncratic. Special education teacher educators need to broaden the candidates' view of the field to see the variety of roles they might play as a special educator. Arranging multiple and varied experiences for candidates, as addressed in Chapter 3, can be helpful in modifying these misconceptions.

Difficulties with Enactment of Skills

Leko (2008) found that teacher candidates had a more difficult time enacting teaching skills learned in their methods classes if they had no opportunity to practice those skills in their field placements. Special education teacher educators need to provide adequate and meaningful practice during training to help candidates gain needed teaching skills. Providing expert role models to candidates can assist in their acquisition of these skills, and use of technology to provide access to these experts can be useful.

Dealing with Complexity

As indicated in this chapter, there are many facets to the job of the special education teacher, and the job is ever changing. Israel (2009) noted that novice special educators particularly have the following challenges: working with paraprofessionals, collaborating with general educators, and learning pedagogical and content knowledge for multiple grade levels and content areas. Additionally, they face issues implementing legal requirements, managing large student caseloads, and dealing with role ambiguity and professional confusion (Gehrke & Murri, 2006).

LOOKING TO THE FUTURE

Special education is a field that seems to always be in a state of change and redefinition. From the early days of having to literally find students with disabilities in order to get them into school, to the current goal of bringing them into the general education curriculum and general education classroom, the role of the special education teacher has changed drastically. We are, as Pugach (2005) stated, continuing to struggle in defining our responsibilities as special educators and what our contributions will be. There continues to be, in both general education and special education teacher preparation, a struggle between student concern and subject matter concern (Darling-Hammond, 2006). In general education, teachers experience this struggle as a tension between subject matter and the interests, experiences, and understanding of students and must do so without losing sight of broader curriculum goals.

In special education, there is greater diversity among students, and a wider range of what is considered to be "the curriculum." Therefore, special education teachers, and by extension special education teacher educators, must connect student goals, whether they are academic, behavioral, or functional, with individual student strengths and needs while simultaneously considering the goals of parents, other teachers, and the general public. We need research on weaving content and pedagogy since the current emphasis is for special education teachers to have both excellent content and excellent pedagogical knowledge. Darling-Hammond (2006) recommends that education be learner and learning centered, which is the basis of constructivist learning and teaching. While this should be a natural fit with special education's goals, the complexities just noted provide challenges to meeting these goals.

Recently, a new model for special education teacher education was proposed (Brownell, Sindelar, Kiely, & Danielson, 2010). These authors noted the current variance in programs and suggested a shift to improve the quality of special education teacher preparation. In reviewing the history of special education teacher preparation, they pointed out that changing views of the profession had been shaped not only by assumptions and research findings about teaching, learning, and disabilities but by political pressures as well. Special education teacher preparation, as noted throughout this book, is in transition, and as preparation varies among categorical, noncategorical, and integrated programs, there remains a need for effective special educators to have knowledge of characteristics, assessment, and interventions. Brownell and colleagues point out that the more we learn about effective teachers, the more accountable we are in special education teacher education. However, as resources and support diminish, reform is more difficult.

Brownell and colleagues (2010) conclude with a description of how the RTI framework can assist us in rethinking special education teacher education and clarifying roles for general education and special education teachers. Like others, they see special education teachers as providing tertiary-level instruction, and collaboratively planning for secondary-level instruction. They further recommend that, in order to target the needs of students more expertly, special education teachers seek advanced preparation focused on the elementary or secondary level.

In his talk about special education teacher education, Meyen (2007) suggested two questions for the next decade: How will we ensure that students with disabilities are taught by teachers who are prepared to offer instruction aligned with standards? Should we begin to prepare special education teacher educators who have doctoral minors or some proficiency in reading, math, and science? I am attempting to address the first of these questions within the pages of this book. The second question is larger, and beyond the scope of this book, but has been addressed by individuals and groups such as Brownell et al. (2005, 2010), Greer and Meyen (2009), Israel (2009), Leko (2008), and Sindelar et al. (2010).

Special Education Teacher Educators

As noted earlier, the transition from teacher to teacher educator is often abrupt (Dinkelman, Margolis, & Sikkenga, 2006) and the jobs are different. However, there is an assumption (Zeichner & Conklin, 2005) that educating teachers doesn't require additional preparation and that there should be automatic carryover from the job of educating younger students. This is actually part of the overall public perception of teaching in general. The prevalent idea is that "you went to school, so you should be able to teach," or "you had teachers so you can be a teacher." As both teachers and teacher educators, we need to take more care of our reputation. Both education and teacher education are worthy areas of study, and require study as well as induction to be done well.

What makes special education teacher education unique includes some of the same issues that face special education. We need to consider ways of helping novice teachers address the unique demands of preparing students with disabilities to successfully pass state assessments, which requires creativity and flexibility on our part, as well as on the part of our candidates. We also need to provide candidates with meaningful and integrated instruction in critical areas: research-validated teaching and assessment practices, legal mandates, and collaborative structures. Special education teacher education also needs to be contextualized within inclusive teaching and educational accountability, and these issues are only slowly affecting teacher education programs (Israel, 2009). These, however, are the current issues—there will be others—and may disappear or decline in importance. Like the candidates they are preparing, special education teacher educators need to be flexible and always learning.

Special education teacher educators are similar to their public school counterparts in one characteristic. Special education teachers are socialized to individualize, be flexible, adjust expectations, and allow for a wide variety of difference. When these individuals (myself included) become special education teacher educators, they are likely to do these things for candidates in their classes—this can be a good thing, or not. On the one hand, it is important to help everyone who wants to be a special education teacher be successful, but it is also important to make sure that they meet high standards. Successful special education teacher educators are able to negotiate these tensions and thus help maintain high standards of both the profession of special educator and the profession of teacher educator.

CHAPTER 5

Special Education Knowledge Base

I not only use all the brains I have, but all that I can borrow.
—WOODROW WILSON

While the wheels of all bureaucracies turn slowly, in school
bureaucracies, many of those wheels have flat tires.
—SUSAN O'HANIANH

The number of books will grow continually, and one can
predict that a time will come when it will be almost as
difficult to learn anything from books as from the direct study
of the whole universe. It will be almost as convenient to search
for some bit of truth concealed in nature as it will be to find it
hidden away in an immense multitude of bound volumes.
—DENIS DIDEROT (1713–1784)

This chapter covers what is currently considered to be best practice in terms of
the content of special education. There are several possible interpretations of what
constitutes "content knowledge" for special education. One can view content as
the actual academic content that is being taught to candidates' students. In that
case, content would cover not only reading, math, science, social studies, and the
arts, but also life skills, social skills, leisure skills, and work skills. This would
include everything from preschool-level skills through skills acquired in high
school and beyond. Addressing this breadth of content is beyond the scope of
this book, and there exist numerous texts on teaching these topics. Current concepts of what special educators need to know range from knowledge of special

instructional techniques to "all of the above." More and more states, in response to recent concepts of "highly qualified," are requiring special educators to be dually certified in special education and at least one area of general education.

Another way to conceptualize the special education knowledge base is to view the actual pedagogy, or manner of teaching the academic or other material, as being the content of special education. The "special education" that is delivered to students in the form of metacognitive skills, problem-solving skills, learning strategies, and so forth. is often in the knowledge bank of the effective special education teacher, along with information about how to make appropriate modifications and accommodations for students so that they can access the curriculum. Finally, knowledge about the role of a special education teacher, including knowledge about the law, procedures, disability characteristics, and so on can be considered an important part of the knowledge base for special education.

This chapter addresses each of these last two aspects of content, as they are important and interwoven areas of knowledge for candidates. These areas are also an important part of what makes special education "special." The chapter also addresses various ways of teaching these content areas, though what is offered here is surely not exhaustive or comprehensive. In particular, techniques addressed here should be considered examples, rather than the only preferred methods. As discussed in Chapter 2, it is impossible to predict what new ways of conveying this information might be available in the future. (See Appendix B for the list of teacher preparation standards developed by CEC.)

The primary role of the special education teacher educator is to assist candidates in preparing to teach their students, and it is up to the special education teacher educator to help candidates help students learn the academic (or other) content. Darling-Hammond (2006) discussed three things that would help general education candidates do this. First, she suggested that there would be an apprenticeship of observation, including modeling by faculty, teaching, and modeling teacher thinking. Good teacher educators, in other words, use modeling of teaching strategies in their own instruction, making transparent their thought processes and their decision making as they teach candidates.

Darling-Hammond (2006) also suggested that teacher educators need to examine candidate thinking and learning in the disciplines. Finally, she suggested that teacher educators need to help candidates develop a curricular perspective on learning. Since special educators are typically expected to be able to teach students across a wide grade/age range (often K–12 or more), the special education teacher educator has the opportunity to help candidates see the "big picture" of the curriculum, and how what is learned in one context or grade will lead to learning later on in another. Further, since it is part of a special educator's job to set annual goals for students, candidates need to learn how to reasonably project into at least the near future. When transition plans are being developed, an even longer range view is necessary.

The factors listed above by Darling-Hammond (2006) are important, but there is even more that special education teachers need to consider—beyond a curricular perspective. Darling-Hammond and Baratz-Snowden (2005) asked in the first chapter of their book *A Good Teacher in Every Classroom*, "What do teachers need to know?" and listed these three items: (1) learners and how they develop/learn within social contexts, (2) subject matter and skills to be taught, and (3) teaching in light of content and learners, informed by assessment and supported by a productive classroom environment.

Within the context of special education there is much variance among these three items. This makes the job of the special education teacher educator that much more difficult and that much more important. Above all, in special education teacher preparation, we need to train *flexible* teachers. Since its passage in 2001, NCLB has required learners to meet uniform expectations, and the Common Core Standards that are currently being considered and adopted by various states also represent uniform curriculum standards. Darling-Hammond (2006) noted, "The more common the expectations for achievement are, the more variable must be the teaching strategies for reaching these goals with a range of learners" (p. 10).

Since special education is responsible for the learners who may have the greatest difficulty achieving the uniform standards of "grade-level" performance and generally represent the outliers of ability, candidates must be provided with a wide range of strategies as well as support for learning and acquiring new teaching skills. Even though the anticipated reauthorization of ESEA might mitigate some of the requirements for every student meeting the same standards at the same rate, it is likely that we are going to continue, at least in the near future, to be operating in an environment of increased expectations for all learners.

What should be part of a curriculum for special education teacher candidates? In part, the answer depends on the overall goals and philosophies of a particular program. As has already been covered in previous chapters, the inclusion of practical field experiences is critical, and it is also important for candidates to understand something about the field they will be a part of and the jobs they may be expected to do. This chapter addresses various features of a special education teacher preparation curriculum that lead to excellent preparation of special education teachers. As noted in the first chapter, there are many different ways to achieve these goals. Meeting them might revolve around specific coursework, fieldwork, independent study, or a combination of ways. I do not intend to be prescriptive as to how teacher educators might go about addressing the features noted here, but will discuss what we know about best practices in these various areas. By and large these examples are drawn from a higher education perspective.

This chapter is divided into five sections. After reviewing the literature on best practices in teacher education, six features of a special education teacher preparation curriculum appeared to be the most important. While the emphasis on one over the other might shift over time, and new features might emerge, these are critical: (1) education about the job (covered in the previous chapter); (2) instruction about student characteristics; (3) leadership education; (4) collaboration; (5) the law, legal responsibilities, and IEPs; and (6) the content being taught and learning to learn (Boe, 2006; Brownell et al., 2003; CEC, 2003, 2009; Darling-Hammond, 2006; Griffin & Pugach, 2007).

A note here about alternative routes to licensure: In some cases, as previously noted, a candidate on a "fast-track" to licensure might only be required to take one or two courses, and perhaps complete a field experience, in order to become licensed to teach (Rosenberg & Sindelar, 2005). In that case, the candidate might only take a class in characteristics of students, methods of teaching, and/or inclusive practices. Therefore which textbook is chosen for these courses might play a critical role in the success of this candidate as it may represent the only reference book the new teacher has. Mamlin (2009) developed a rubric to evaluate texts to determine how completely these important issues were covered (see Figure 5.1). CEC standards for teachers, as well as other literature reviewed in this book, helped set standards for evaluating the texts (Boe, 2006; Brownell et al., 2003; CEC, 2003, 2009; Darling-Hammond, 2006; Griffin & Pugach, 2007). In the review of 28 textbooks (Introduction to Special Education, Methods, and Inclusion texts), only a few texts were discovered that addressed all of these items. Figure 5.2 contains the list of texts reviewed. Inclusion texts appeared to be the most comprehensive, so it was recommended from that study that if candidates are only going to take one course, an inclusion course, or at least use of an inclusion textbook, might be the best choice.

The following sections address these five areas of the special education knowledge base (education about the job was the topic of Chapter 4), noting why each is considered to be an important part of curriculum, and addressing some current best practices in conveying this information to candidates.

FEATURE 1: INSTRUCTION ABOUT STUDENT CHARACTERISTICS

It is important for candidates to understand various disability categories, and how students might be identified as having one or more of these disabilities. This is usually the starting point for candidates in special education programs, typically constructed as one or more "introduction to—" courses. In such courses, basic information is covered regarding the definitions of the 13 federally defined categories, typical approaches to teaching students who have those labels, and some information about current issues in the field.

There are several approaches special education teacher educators may choose to take when teaching such courses. A variety of factors, including the overall goals of the program and where this course fits into the curriculum, should be considered in determining the best choice. Some programs may offer multiple

Book title: _____

Author: _____

Year of publication: _____

Feature	Number of pages/chapters devoted	Type of information (text, activities, info boxes, etc.)	Other information
Diversity			
Inclusion			
What does a special ed teacher do?			
History of education			
History of special education			
Student characteristics (usually by disability category)			*Which categories? All 13? Are some missing? Gifted included?*
Ethics and professional standards			
Leadership skills			
Collaboration			
Laws			
IEPs			
Academic content: Reading			
Academic content: Writing			
Academic content: Math			
Academic content: Science			
Academic content: Social studies			
Academic content: Other			
Social skills instruction			
Assessment			

FIGURE 5.1. Rubric for textbook evaluation.

Inclusion

Choate, J. S. (2004). *Successful inclusive teaching* (4th ed.). Upper Saddle River, NJ: Merrill/ Prentice Hall.

Freund, L., & Rich, R. (2005). *Teaching students with learning problems in the inclusive classroom.* Upper Saddle River, NJ: Merrill/Prentice Hall.

Friend, M., & Bursuck, W. D. (2009). *Including students with special needs* (5th ed.). Upper Saddle River, NJ: Merrill/Prentice Hall.

Mastropieri, M. A., & Scruggs, T. E. (2010). *The inclusive classroom* (4th ed.). Upper Saddle River, NJ: Merrill/Prentice Hall.

Salend, S. J. (2008). *Creating inclusive classrooms* (6th ed.). Upper Saddle River, NJ: Merrill/ Prentice Hall.

Smith, T. E. C., Polloway, E. A., Patton, J. R., & Dowdy, C. A. (2008). *Teaching students with special needs in inclusive settings* (5th ed.). Upper Saddle River, NJ: Merrill/Prentice Hall.

Introduction to Exceptional Children

Friend, M. (2008). *Special education: Contemporary perspectives for school professionals.* Upper Saddle River, NJ: Merrill/Prentice Hall.

Gargiulo, R. M. (2006). *Special education in contemporary society* (2nd ed.). Belmont, CA: Thompson/Wadsworth.

Hallahan, D. P., Kauffman, J. M., & Pullen, P. C. (2009). *Exceptional learners: An introduction to special education* (11th ed.). Upper Saddle River, NJ: Merrill/Prentice Hall.

Heward, W. L. (2009). *Exceptional children: An introduction to special education* (9th ed.). Upper Saddle River, NJ: Merrill/Prentice Hall.

Hunt, N., & Marshall, K. (2005). *Exceptional children and youth* (4th ed.). Boston: Houghton Mifflin.

Kirk, S., Gallagher, J. J., Anastasiow, N. J., & Coleman, M. R. (2006). *Educating exceptional children* (11th ed.). Boston: Houghton Mifflin.

Meyen, E., & Bui, Y. (2007). *Exceptional children in today's schools: What teachers need to know* (4th ed.). Denver: Love.

Raymond, E. B. (2008). *Learners with mild disabilities: A characteristics approach* (3rd ed.). Upper Saddle River, NJ: Merrill/Prentice Hall.

Rosenberg, M. S., Westling, D. L., & McLeskey, J. (2008). *Special education for today's teachers: An introduction.* Upper Saddle River, NJ: Merrill/Prentice Hall.

Smith, D. D. (2007). *Introduction to special education: Making a difference* (6th ed.). Upper Saddle River, NJ: Merrill/Prentice Hall.

Stichter, J. P., Conroy, M. A., & Kauffmann, J. M. (2008). *An introduction to students with high- incidence disabilities.* Upper Saddle River, NJ: Merrill/Prentice Hall.

Taylor, R., Smiley, L., & Richards, S. (2009). *Exceptional students: Preparing teachers for the 21st century.* New York: McGraw-Hill.

Turnbull, A. P., Turnbull, H. R., & Wehmeyer, M. L. (2007). *Exceptional lives: Special education in today's schools* (5th ed.). Upper Saddle River, NJ: Merrill/Prentice Hall.

Werts, M. G., Culatta, R. A., & Tompkins, J. R. (2007). *Fundamentals of special education: What every teacher needs to know* (3rd ed.). Upper Saddle River, NJ: Merrill/Prentice Hall.

(cont.)

FIGURE 5.2. Textbooks evaluated by Mamlin (2009).

Methods

Henley, M. R., Algozzine, R. F., & Ramsey, R. S. (2009). *Characteristics of and strategies for teaching students with mild disabilities* (6th ed.). Upper Saddle River, NJ: Merrill/Prentice Hall.

Mercer, C. D., & Mercer, A. R. (2005). *Teaching students with learning problems* (7th ed.). Upper Saddle River, NJ: Merrill/Prentice Hall.

Olson, J. L., Platt, J. C., & Dieker, L. A. (2008). *Teaching children and adolescents with special needs* (5th ed.). Upper Saddle River, NJ: Merrill/Prentice Hall.

Polloway, E. A., Patton, J. R., & Serna, L. (2008). *Strategies for teaching learners with special needs* (9th ed.). Upper Saddle River, NJ: Merrill/Prentice Hall.

Prater, M. A. (2007). *Teaching strategies for students with mild to moderate disabilities.* Upper Saddle River, NJ: Merrill/Prentice Hall.

Sabornie, E. J., & deBettencourt, L. U. (2009). *Teaching students with mild and high-incidence disabilities at the secondary level* (3rd ed.). Upper Saddle River, NJ: Merrill/Prentice Hall.

Snell, M. E., & Brown, F. (2006). *Instruction of students with severe disabilities* (6th ed.). Upper Saddle River, NJ: Merrill/Prentice Hall.

Vaughn, S., & Bos, C. S. (2009). *Strategies for teaching students with learning and behavior problems* (7th ed.). Upper Saddle River, NJ: Merrill/Prentice Hall.

FIGURE 5.2. *(cont.)*

"characteristics" courses—one that covers the field of special education in general, then others that focus on particular disability areas. If that is the case in the program you are involved in, you can use the first introduction course as a "preview of coming attractions," while spending a bit more time on areas that won't be covered later on. When providing candidates with this basic information, the special education teacher educator has the opportunity to bring in professionals, colleagues, and parents as guests. Additionally, a field component to the course might be required, even volunteer work in various settings with infants, students, or adults with disabilities. Including other voices can add different perspectives and provide information to candidates about various job opportunities.

One common way that books about student characteristics are laid out, particularly those that cover a range of disabilities, is by covering "a disability a week." However, it is often preferable to teach using larger concepts such as cognitive differences, physical differences, and medical needs, for example, rather than running through the list of the 13 categories. A primary rationale for this approach is that in public schools, it is rare to find students grouped by category. Rather, they are more likely (and more appropriately) to be grouped by needs. Further, speaking about students according to their needs rather than their label will help emphasize that once a student has a label then it is their needs that should be addressed, regardless of label. On the other hand, teachers do need to be aware of the different categories and what leads to decisions to use one label over another for a particular student. It should also be pointed out that labels do provide some information to teachers and others.

Teaching candidates about the categories used in special education, then, can become a careful balancing act. The following questions may be addressed to help guide instruction: What are the common characteristics of each category? What are the common instructional approaches used in local schools for students with this disability label? What are the approaches that are recommended by the professional literature? What are the common misconceptions about particular categories? What can candidates do to help correct these misconceptions? Answering each of these questions within an Introduction to Special Education course can assist candidates in seeing the differences as well as the commonalities across categories. Students may be guided to keep this information in a graphic organizer such as Figure 5.3. The 13 categories are listed in that figure in the order of probability of their inclusion in general education classrooms (USDOE, 2007), but the order in which they are introduced in the course might be followed just as well. This should help candidates organize and learn the large amount of information they need to master.

Care should also be taken to provide correct information about each disability category the text uses and to determine whether it is accurate. For example, a colleague of mine who teaches in the area of visual impairment checked several Introduction to Special Education books his graduate candidates had been exposed to in their previous special education instruction. Glancing through the chapters on visual impairment, he noted outdated and in some cases inaccurate information. Most special education teacher educators are not experts in every area of special education, so it would be in the candidates' best interests to make sure that the best possible information is being presented.

Battling Misconceptions

How do we correct misconceptions about various categories? Like the general public, teacher candidates may have certain misconceptions about people with disabilities. Commonly held beliefs are often supported by the media as well as general educators. People may generalize from a single, or very few, personal examples. These misconceptions may include ideas about frequency and nature of disabilities, settings where students are educated, general outcomes of special education students, and what is legally required. One way to address these is to confront them directly. For example, when a candidate states "All students have a disability," point out that most students fall in the "normal range"—hence the concept of "normal." Or a student may equate having Down syndrome with having severe mental retardation. The teacher educator should point out that individuals with Down syndrome have a range of cognitive abilities, and that knowing that a student has Down syndrome does not provide enough information to make such a judgment.

One error in teaching an introductory class, especially with faculty who feel ill prepared to teach about every category, is to assign candidates to cover different categories and report on these to the rest of the class. If this were sufficient, then simply reading a good textbook should be all that would be required. The

Disability label	Common characteristics	Common instructional approaches		Common misconceptions	What I can do to correct misconceptions
		Used in local schools	Recommended by literature		
Speech–language					
Developmental delay					
Visual impairment					
Other health impairments					
Learning disabilities					
Orthopedic impairment					
Hearing impairment					
Traumatic brain injury					
Emotional disorders					
Autism					
Deaf/blindness					
Intellectual disabilities					
Multiple disabilities					

FIGURE 5.3. Disability labels used by IDEIA, characteristics, instructional approaches, and misconceptions. These are listed in the order of probability that students with these labels are served in general education classrooms (USDOE, 2007).

difficulties with this approach may seem obvious—candidates may not have the background to find information that is reliable, accurate, or up to date. If candidates are enrolled in an introductory course, the assumption can be made that they have insufficient accurate background knowledge, but may have quite a bit of idiosyncratic knowledge, outdated knowledge, or misinformation. They very likely do not have the breadth of knowledge a seasoned special education teacher would have. The instructors for these courses need to take charge of the information that will be presented. If there is an area where an instructor does not feel comfortable, an expert from outside can be brought in—a local schoolteacher who teaches students in this population, another faculty member whose expertise is in the area, a parent, or even a student who has that disability.

Another teaching strategy for Introduction as well as many other courses, is the use of cases. Several texts may include case studies either as part of the main text or in supplemental materials. Alternatively, cases can be found elsewhere, such as among the IRIS resources (*iris.peabody.vanderbilt.edu*). The University of South Florida (*cases.coedu.usf.edu/default.htm*) also has a good collection of cases which can be searched by either topic or CEC competency standards. Cases instructors might select from these or other sources range from simple, one-issue ideas to complex cases, depending on the particular goals of the instructor.

In any case, in an Introduction to Special Education class, the main questions candidates have are likely to be (1) "Who counts as disabled?" and (2) "What do I do with them in my classroom?" The second question is probably the more important and likely beyond the scope of a single term's introductory course. However, teacher educators should include at least a few ideas and examples to provide context for candidates. The answer to the first question can be largely addressed by helping candidates understand the IEP process—how a student comes to be identified by the IEP team as being in need of special education services. This will be covered later in this chapter.

FEATURE 2: LEADERSHIP EDUCATION

Leadership education, similar in many ways to education about teaching, is a more focused look at one aspect of the special educator's job. Special educators are likely default leaders in their schools from day one, and may be the most knowledgeable persons in the building about special education even as new teachers. In some schools, there may be just one special educator assigned to the school. This puts novice teachers as well as experienced teachers in the position of searching out mentors, both inside and outside the school building. In teacher preparation programs, we should provide guidance to candidates about how to do this. As teacher educators, we need to help candidates understand how to communicate effectively and collaborate with administrators, fellow teachers, and others.

McLaughlin and Nolet (2004) listed five things that every principal needs to know about special education: (1) legal foundations of special education, (2) that special education is essentially about matching instructional practices to individual needs (rather than a label), (3) that special education is not a particular place, but a description of a set of services, (4) how to meaningfully include students with IEPs in required assessments, and (5) how to create a schoolwide climate that is supportive of special education. While it would be optimal if all principals were familiar with these concepts and were expert in making them happen, it is unfortunately too often not the case. That doesn't mean that these ideas are unimportant, however. Therefore, the special educators present in the building need to be capable of tactfully and professionally making sure that their principals understand these concepts. The paragraphs below contain suggestions for teacher educators who want to help candidates gain the skills to address these issues with their current/future principals.

Legal Foundations

Most principals are aware that there are "legal" aspects to special education. However, novice principals, or those without a good grounding in special education, may be inclined to react to these legalities with fear. Likewise, new special education teachers—as well as some seasoned teachers—at times seem to see every encounter with an IEP team, a parent, or another teacher as a lawsuit waiting to happen. Of course, everyone needs to be aware of their legal responsibilities, but acting out of fear is not helpful. Teacher educators should emphasize to candidates that if they understand their job, and do it with integrity and in good faith, the chances of a "lawsuit" are considerably lessened. According to Zirkel and Gischlar (2008), approximately .08% (180/10,000) of students had cases adjudicated in 2005.

To increase the chances of everything going smoothly, special education teachers need to do everything in their power to make sure that the appropriate people come together to make decisions about students. This might go beyond the required set of IEP team members to include other teachers or interested adults and the student before reaching transition age. They also need to do all possible to make sure that the agreed-upon services for their students are being adequately delivered. However, it does no one any good to fret about minor disruptions in service. Candidates need to be assured that if something happens that is beyond their control, and they have documented what they were able to do about situations, then they are in a stronger position.

Special Education Is a Description of a Set of Services

This may be another difficult concept for special education teacher educators to get across to candidates, and for candidates to get across to their principals.

For the early part of special education's history, it was common for schools to have self-contained settings which were labeled by disability. There would be, for example, a self-contained "LD class," a self-contained "MR class," and a self-contained "ED class," all within the same school, each of them having students with a large range of ages and needs that the teachers of those classes were responsible for. Many special education teacher educators are familiar with this configuration from their own experiences, and might feel that it was a successful situation for their students. Even now, there are classrooms referred to as "the autistic classroom" or teachers referred to as "the intellectual disabilities teacher." It is part of our role as special education teacher educators to point out the problems in describing classrooms and teachers in this way, as it serves to maintain outmoded and outdated practices. Helping our candidates change their language, and modeling appropriate language for them, will eventually assist in changing practice in the schools and society in general.

Instead of making distinctions by disability labels, it is now more likely and considered best practice to have teachers who work with students according to what their IEP goals are, and have students grouped according to those goals and needs. It is also likely that the special education teachers would be helping their students with these goals within the context of the general education classroom. Candidates, then, need to be able to communicate to principals and teachers that students with IEPs are students first—and that as long as the services are being delivered, it does not have to be the special education teacher who does it. The goals can be addressed by the general education teacher, the school counselor, or others. What is important is that the special services are delivered, and that the special education teacher assures that this happens. The clearer that the IEP is about who, when, and where the special education takes place, the easier this will be.

Matching Instructional Practices to Individual Needs (Rather Than a Label)

Candidates must understand that it is the I in IEP that is the most important letter. Probably one of the most challenging concepts to get across to candidates is that while labeling students with disabilities is important, the label does not drive decisions made in IEP meetings. The label merely provides access to appropriate services. Figure 5.4 provides an illustration that may help explain this concept. To complete the illustration, one could imagine an exit door as well, where students leave when they graduate, age out, or no longer need special education services.

This concept can be difficult for candidates, especially as they start learning about pre-referral and placement procedures. IDEIA requires, as have all laws back to Public Law 94-142, that a student be given one or more disability labels. It seems logical, then, that the disability label itself would indicate or direct what the rest of the IEP would contain, including goals, objectives, placement, related

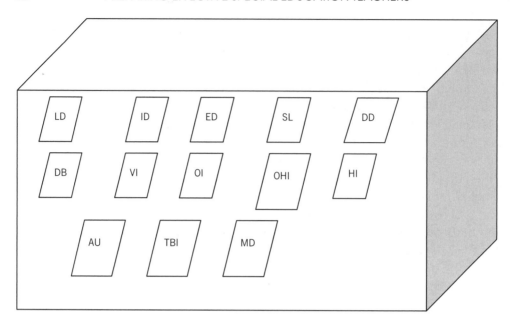

FIGURE 5.4. Graphical representation of the relation of special education labels to IEPs. Students with disabilities each go in their own door, but are all in the "same box." The instructor can use this as a partial illustration of how an individual, upon receiving a special education label, enters into the "world of special education" (inside the box). There, the IEP is written without regard to "which door" the student entered.

services, and more. However, choosing a particular label is of relatively minor importance in the process. More important is using a student's current levels of performance to plan appropriate goals and an appropriate IEP.

Meaningfully Including Students in Required Assessments

Teacher educators need to stay abreast of current assessment practices in general as well as special education. Information about local practices would probably be most meaningful to candidates, but it is also important to be able to give the state and national view of how assessments are being carried out. As this book is being written, the overall assessment landscape is changing, as NCLB is being re-formed and re-conceptualized as the ESEA. The CEC, among other professional organizations, is seeking to influence this reauthorization, just as they have in the past (see *www.cec.sped.org/Content/NavigationMenu/PolicyAdvocacy/ CECPolicyResources/NoChildLeftBehind/CEC_2010_ESEA_Policy_WEB.pdf*). Candidates must understand that their main concern should be the meaningfulness of the assessment. Does the assessment give meaningful information to the teacher, the school, the public? The best assessments, of course, would do all three.

One of the difficulties with the required assessments under NCLB has been the lack of useful information it provides about students in special education. One of the primary reasons that students are in need of a special education is that they are academically behind their peers. The fact that they continue to be behind is merely an indication that they still need special education services and typically comes as no surprise to anyone who is familiar with the students. If a majority of special education students are passing grade-level tests, then one might logically question the meaningfulness of "grade level" and what it means for students in general education or whether those students are appropriately considered to have special education needs.

What has occurred under NCLB is that all students are given tests based on their chronological /current grade placement. If, for example, a fifth-grader is considered to be at a second-grade level at the start of fifth grade, it should be reasonable to expect him or her to be at a third-grade level at the end of the year. Given a third-grade-level test, stakeholders could determine whether meaningful progress was made at the end of the year. Given a fifth-grade-level test, all we know is that the student is still behind. This inequity might well be addressed in the ESEA reauthorization. In any case, special education teacher educators, candidates, and practicing teachers need to do all they can to have assessments that provide meaningful information. This will often require providing students with assessments that are selected on an individual basis. Therefore, we need to provide candidates with much more extensive information about both formal and informal assessments.

Helping Create a Schoolwide Climate That Is Supportive of Special Education

Teacher educators should help candidates understand how to assist in developing a supportive climate for themselves and their students. Some of this work is helping candidates understand the nuances of how to present themselves in their schools. School leaders can also assist in this goal, as they help both general educators and special educators build collaborative skills, including providing adequate time and resources to assist them in working together (McLaughlin & Nolet, 2004).

Leadership arises in nearly every aspect of a special education teacher's job description. It is part of the CEC competencies and is expected to be addressed at every point in a special education teacher's career. Even as a beginning teacher, the special education teacher is expected to take the lead in IEP meetings, and as a specialist might be called upon to provide staff development for the faculty at the school or district level. Therefore, in preparation programs, candidates should be given the opportunity to practice these skills and receive feedback which will help them to become more effective communicators and leaders. Candidates should also be encouraged to take positions on issues that are important to the field, and defend those positions with reliable and valid information as indicated by some of the ideas mentioned here.

FEATURE 3: COLLABORATION

Collaboration across disciplines is an important feature of exemplary programs (Brownell et al., 2003). This includes collaboration with general education, and taking advantage of co-teaching opportunities. Indeed, a major aspect of the job of a special education teacher is working with faculty in other disciplines. Keeping in mind that modeling is important in teacher education, we in special education teacher education also need to collaborate with teacher education and other faculty. Brownell et al. (2003) identified collaboration across disciplines as an important feature of exemplary programs. This includes collaboration with general education, as well as taking advantage of co-teaching opportunities.

As inclusion is more common in schools, special education teachers (and general education teachers) will be expected to know how to collaborate effectively, and how to negotiate different collaborative opportunities differently (Friend, 2007). When candidates have the opportunity to see us modeling co-teaching, valuing each other's contributions, and learning from each other, then they may be more likely to see collaboration as a possibility for them in their own teaching positions. There are, of course, many roadblocks in universities to doing this, not the least of which is coming to terms with different philosophies and emphases of programs.

These are the same struggles our candidates will be faced with, and it would be educative to help them see ways to negotiate dilemmas. Another issue is that in many dual-license programs, content in special education tends to get short shrift. Dual-license programs still need to provide enough information and practice to assure that candidates are addressing all the skills and knowledge in this chapter. Faculty need to assure that candidates are getting what they need in our programs, while staying clear of unnecessary "turf wars."

One way to promote and model collaboration when collaboration with other faculty has too many roadblocks is to invite individuals who work in local schools to work with you in teaching candidates. If doctoral students are available at the university, in special education, leadership, educational psychology, or another appropriate program, they might be asked to collaborate in teaching a course. If not, local teachers, principals, or other district personnel might be invited to assist. It is helpful if some money is available, but it may require no more than your respect for their expertise and asking them to share it with candidates. Special education teacher educators can also barter services with local school professionals, agreeing to provide staff development or other support for their employees.

When teaching about collaboration, aside from modeling, giving candidates opportunities to practice collaborative skills is important. These may include use of case studies, role playing, simulations, and field experiences. For example, Bradley and Monda-Amaya (2005) described instruction designed to help preservice teachers understand, analyze, and take steps toward resolving teacher–teacher conflicts. They used a curriculum package which presented vignettes for candidates to respond to, which potentially helped candidates change their perspectives toward future conflicts. If collaborative field experiences are arranged, care should be taken that candidates are seeing best practices in collaboration being modeled. Supervision should be done by teacher educators who themselves have expertise in collaborative teaching, whether they are from a special or general education background. This is addressed in more detail in Chapter 3.

In terms of specific collaborative skills which candidates need to practice, we should think about the various groups with whom collaboration is necessary.

The Inclusion Dilemma

The biggest barrier to inclusion is inclusion as practiced in many of our schools today. I have been observing teachers and schools since the late 1980s in several states and school districts in those states. Many teachers and principals have told me they are "doing inclusion," or "teaching inclusion." However, most times they are going about their work without the training, effort, and expertise required. It is as if they consider "doing inclusion" to be an "event" that administrators can decide will happen in their schools, like a decision about when lunch will be served or where the busses will unload. A more helpful way to think of inclusion is as a way of educating all students in a school, and to remember that there may be cases where students are separated for specific instruction, or therapies that are not appropriate for larger groups. A decision to promote inclusive practices implies a need for all teachers in the school to come to a mutual understanding about their students. The notion that "inclusion" is something that a special educator does actually works against the ideas of inclusive practices and can set practices back.

In many cases, evidence of teaching practices that truly include all students is missing. I investigated (Mamlin, 1999) inclusive practices in a school that not only purported to be "doing inclusion" but was receiving technical support from a university to help them increase inclusive practices. In that school, though, all students with special needs were separated for all of their academic instruction. In spite of this, the teachers, the principal, and other staff at the school consistently referred to "the inclusion program."

Clearly teacher education plays an important role in modifying practices in the schools. As we educate candidates, we need to be careful about how we refer to inclusion, and be quite clear that it is a way to think about educating all students in a school, and involves all professionals in a school. Special education candidates and general education candidates (as well as administrator candidates) can benefit from coursework about inclusive practices. The more we can advocate for the education of all students in a school, the better schools will be.

Friend and Cook (2010) defined collaboration as follows: "Interpersonal *collaboration* is a style for direct interaction between at least two co-equal parties, voluntarily engaged in shared decision making, as they work toward a common goal" (p. 7). Considering all the co-equal parties who are potential collaborators, we should help our candidates gain skills in collaborating with general education teachers, administrators, and other professionals in the schools (e.g., therapists, counselors, other specialists). Likewise, we should help them learn collaborative skills with para-educators, families, and community members. Some candidates will need more practice and direct instruction than others, but most people can find areas of collaboration in which they want to improve their skills.

FEATURE 4: THE LAW, IEPs, AND LEGAL RESPONSIBILITIES

I have long maintained, and tried to convince teacher candidates whom I instruct, that "paperwork is your friend." This is certainly not a commonly held belief, however. We must help teacher candidates understand the importance of good documentation, not just to cover legal responsibilities, but to improve their instruction and their communication with others. Whether LEAs in the area use computer-assisted IEP software, or write plans by hand, candidates need to see IEP development as something beyond "more paperwork."

As special education teacher educators, we need to value IEPs and their meaningfulness and usefulness in designing a curriculum for special education students. The more exposure to and practice with the IEP process that can be a part of a teacher education program, the more comfortable candidates will be with what is required as they lead IEP meetings. In her dissertation, Gavins (2007) discovered that even experienced special education teachers (with ten or more years' experience) did not necessarily write relevant and technically adequate IEPs. However, newer teachers (one to two years' experience) in her study had a wider range of difficulties. She found that ability to write adequate IEPs developed along a continuum, and that staff development should likely continue beyond the first few years of teaching experience. Providing more practice in a teacher preparation program is analogous to the necessity of field experiences to teaching practice. However, issues of student confidentiality can stand in the way of candidates receiving ample and varied practice in IEP development and leadership on IEP teams.

One way to help provide more practice, and to involve other faculty and candidates, is to create role-playing situations. In one large program, the special education faculty invited other education faculty and staff and general education candidates to participate in mock IEP meetings. Candidates were assigned the role of "special education teacher," and given a case study of a student they were meeting about. The case studies were actual local cases, with the names and other identifying information redacted. Other participants were given roles of parent, student, general education teacher, principal, and others. Candidates were thus able to practice their communication and collaboration skills in a low-risk environment, with special education faculty available to address concerns and questions (Werts et al., 2002). This helped take some of the mystery out of the process when they atttended meetings as interns or student teachers, and then in beginning practice.

As more attention is paid to reducing unnecessary paperwork, it should be a logical outcome that remaining paperwork is more useful and necessary. Unfortunately, special educators and other educators tend to see *all* paperwork as a bad thing, and may "throw the baby out with the bathwater." There is a danger of eliminating some necessary paperwork in the quest to cut down on paperwork. For example, currently, the use of short-term objectives is not required for some IEPs (IDEIA, 2004). Eliminating short-term objectives from the IEP eliminates some of the communicative value of the IEP. Parents and others could monitor ongoing progress of a student, and teachers could communicate progress in a more meaningful way with the short-term objectives in place. With annual goals, special education teachers have to create their own "roadmaps" for reaching those goals, instead of taking advantage of the wisdom of the IEP team to help them lay out short-term goals.

Aside from the IDEIA, and the IEP, which is at the heart of special education practice, special education candidates need to understand other laws and mandates that influence their practice. Special education teacher educators should ensure that candidates understand the basic tenets of Section 504 of the Rehabilitation Act of 1973 and help candidates learn to communicate with parents and other professionals about the similarities and differences between Section 504 and the IDEIA. Likewise, an understanding of the ADA (2009) is important. Finally, like all teachers, an understanding of the ESEA is critical. Special education teacher educators need to address the implications of the ESEA and other laws for special education teachers and students.

FEATURE 5: THE CONTENT BEING TAUGHT AND LEARNING TO LEARN

It is one thing to understand the core curriculum of a grade level, a school, or even the entire K–12 curriculum. In special education, though, it is our candidates' job to know how to deliver that curriculum in a way that special education students can not only access it, but progress in it, as required by both the IDEIA and the ESEA. Special education programs need to address how they will deal with the issue of making sure our candidates can become highly qualified (or highly effective), if necessary, for their job. There are various ways to do this, and each program's solution will have to fit the needs of the candidate, the institution of higher education, and the state. At a minimum, however, our

Scaffolding Teaching

In my role as a special education teacher educator, I often have students who, though enthusiastic about teaching students with disabilities, really have little to no prior knowledge about how to go about teaching a lesson. As their professor for any number of "methods" classes, one of my goals is to help them create lesson and unit plans that both communicate to me (or some other outsider who might judge them, such as a principal, substitute, or coworker) and are useful for themselves as they teach. Basically, I am interested in their having a good, measureable behavioral objective, a plan for introducing their lesson, providing direct instruction, scaffolding, guided practice, and wrapping up. I also want them to address how the lesson is generalizable. In fact, if they are unable to articulate how the lesson is generalizable I recommend that they not teach it. There is only so much time to provide an education, and their learners are by definition inefficient at learning, so why waste time if the instructor doesn't know why the lesson is occurring? Finally, I want them to provide information about how they will measure the success (or not) of their students in meeting their behavioral objectives.

To begin the discussion of teaching, we first discuss their own perceptions of what makes an effective teacher. To help them do this, I ask them to think about the best teacher they have ever had, from kindergarten through college, and to list a few characteristics of that person that made them effective. Then they share these perceptions in small groups, and come up with a list of effective teaching behaviors. We then combine all those lists into one large list posted where everyone can see it, and compare that list with a list of effective teaching behaviors indicated by current research. Often there will be some overlap in these two lists, but not much. For example, the notion of good classroom management may show up on both lists, but more nonobservable characteristics such as "My first grade teacher really cared about all the students" would only show up on the student-generated list. We then discuss how all these attributes from both lists are important, but that in my role as a teacher educator, I can only help them with certain skills. Hopefully they have already developed and will continue to develop skills of empathy, caring, a good sense of humor, and the like.

At this point I often also share with the candidates various forms that may be used by local districts or the state to evaluate teachers. These are generally available online, and may also mirror what is used by supervisors and cooperating teachers in student teaching. This helps students see the relationships between effective teaching and the observation forms.

Next, to introduce the idea of teaching, and following the steps that I want them to use when they teach, I first model how I teach a lesson. I am a traditional square dance caller, and so I bring in recorded music, teach my candidates a simple dance, and then have them do it. We then talk about my teaching behavior—they note what was effective and (perhaps) ineffective in my teaching, and what made the task easier or more difficult for some of them (such as having prior knowledge or skills that they could relate to the task). I also tell them what my goal was for them, and ask them if I have a way to know whether or not they had met that goal.

(cont.)

I then ask the candidates to think of something they know how to do, that might be interesting to other adults to learn, that they could then teach to a group of their peers—about a 10- to 15-minute lesson total. I give them examples of things students have taught in the past, and have a few rules about what is not allowable. For example, students might teach a sports skill (especially if the weather is likely to be nice), a card trick, how to say some words or phrases in a foreign language, or how to do a craft that adults enjoy (such as knitting). Examples of things that aren't allowed are foreign languages commonly taught in high schools, or the American Sign Language, since too many peers will already have some facility with these skills before they begin teaching. They also need to provide enough materials for the group to use, which may limit what they choose to teach. The main objective for this portion of my unit is that candidates come up with a goal, and a way to tell whether their students for this exercise have met that goal. When the students have had a chance to teach their skills to one another, we then reconvene and discuss how it went. The candidates can offer one another critiques, and we can address whether they had goals, and if they were able to tell whether or not their students met their goals.

From this point, the next class session will begin the discussions of how to write a good, measureable, behavioral objective for their future (or current) K–12 students. These are related to, but not the same as, IEP objectives, in that these are for much shorter periods of time. Some candidates may find this helpful, and others may find it confusing. In either case, it is important to understand the relationship.

The next step in the process of learning to teach is to create a lesson plan for the first time. For this initial practice, I put the candidates in groups of no more than four. I go over the format I require (such as in Figure 5.5) and provide them with a general objective for their lesson, along with the standard state goal it aligns with. I bring in various materials they might choose to use to teach the lesson (e.g., math manipulatives for a math lesson) and encourage them to work together to create a single, well-written, well-thought-out lesson plan. After the group has successfully completed a lesson plan, each member is then ready to write his or her own plans. Nevertheless, there are always candidates who need further scaffolding, and I use a mastery learning model that allows candidates to rewrite their plans until they are satisfied with them.

Before I began using this process to introduce objectives, measurement of those objectives, and the process of teaching, I found that my candidates were lost, especially initially, when asked to create lesson plans on their own. I found that many prerequisite skills were missing, ones I assumed they already had. By slowing down a bit in how I introduced the idea of writing lesson plans, I ended up with better-quality plans that the candidates were able to make real use of when they went out into the schools for their practicum placements.

candidates need to have a grasp on reading/literacy, mathematics, science, and social studies goals for the general education peers of their students. They then need to know how to help their students progress toward those same general education goals.

One way to approach an understanding of course content might be to collaborate with general education teachers around a course organizer such as one of the approaches developed by Lenz, Deshler, and Kissam (2004) in their text *Teaching Content to All: Evidence-Based Inclusive Practices in Middle and Secondary Schools*. In this approach to course planning, the teachers discuss the "big picture" of the course, what content should be mastered by all learners, what content most learners should master, and what content will be learned by fewer learners. Teachers use this plan to help decide how material will be learned, and how performance will be assessed. Their approach was developed for middle and high school environments, but could easily be adapted for elementary schools as well.

In teacher education, I recommend that we use a single, agreed-upon format for creating lesson plans in our individual programs. However, candidates need to be made aware that there may be other forms required or formats suggested by school districts they work in. If one format can be developed and agreed upon among teacher educators in a program, several advantages can be realized. The format can reflect the underlying philosophy or perspective of the program. Candidates are better able to focus on the content of the lesson once they have mastered the format. Assessing completeness and quality of plans is easier for teacher education faculty as well, since there will be a specific place for each element. One example of such a format is presented in Figure 5.5.

A question that often arises among methods faculty and their students is about what level of detail should be required in a plan. For candidates, and novice teachers, especially if the plans are for nonexistent classrooms as is often the case with undergraduates, more detail is better. This allows candidates to think through the entire process of teaching a lesson, and allows instructors to know what candidates are thinking. When I teach these classes, I use the phrase "drop-dead lesson plans." I coined this phrase to illustrate to candidates that the plans should contain enough detail that if the candidate were to "drop dead," after a moment of silence, another person could pick up the lesson plan and teach the lesson just the way it was intended. This may be too morose for some instructors and some candidates, but I have used it for over two decades, and with the correct delivery, it can make the point.

Learning Strategies

Knowledge of learning strategies, task analysis, adaptive technology, and other modifications and accommodations is also necessary for our candidates. It is clear that the vast majority of students receiving special education services are inefficient learners. If they were progressing as expected, then they would not need

Part of lesson	Comments/guidance on how to complete
Lesson plan topic	For example: math, reading, writing, social skills.
Source	Here is where to list where I got the idea for this plan. Some possibilities would be from books, other teachers, or websites. If it's a website, I must give the url. There's a chance I could have thought of it myself. In that case, I am the source.
Students	Here is where I will tell how many students I have who have IEPs, as well as a brief description of how many other students are present. I will also say what grade they are in, and provide other pertinent information.
Lesson location/time	Here is where I will say whether the location is a general education classroom or a resource room or elsewhere. It may happen in a computer lab somewhere else. If it's an elementary (K–8) plan, I will plan for 45 minutes. If it's a secondary (9–12) plan, I will plan for 90 minutes. (*Note:* 90 minutes is the typical time for class periods in North Carolina high schools.) If the lesson will be in a general education classroom, I have to remember the following: • Plan for the special education teacher and the general education teacher to share responsibility. • Indicate how I will plan for and accommodate the students with IEPs who are in the class.
State curriculum goals	Here I will list the standard curriculum goals that will be addressed partially by this lesson. I will not forget to write the grade level(s) that the goal is intended for.
Prerequisite skills	This should be a list. The question I need to answer here is: What things can the students already do which will help them in this lesson? Also, what have they already done in preparation for the lesson? (For example, if they've already read the first three chapters of a book and this lesson begins with Chapter 4.) I need to write *skills* rather than generalities.
Behavioral objectives	I will list these if I have more than one. Each objective is one sentence long and has all four parts. I don't need to say things in the objective about *why* it is the objective. I should not include things in the objective that are not observable.
Materials	I will list these. I don't have to list the teacher and student materials separately, unless we need different things. Materials commonly found in the classroom need not be listed (e.g., desks, paper, pens, pencils, whiteboard, etc.).
Lesson body	I want to make this part easy to read, so when I refer to it while I'm teaching, I can easily find my place.
Beginning of lesson: Preview/review	What's the first thing I say/do with the class? I probably should *activate prior knowledge* by asking them if they remember what we did last time. I should also give them a preview of what we'll be doing today. I might choose to write an agenda on the board.

(cont.)

FIGURE 5.5. Sample lesson plan format. When candidates are learning to create lesson plans, it is useful to have a format for them to follow. This is an example of one I have used in an undergraduate preparation program. It includes guidance I give students as part of direct instruction as well as in writing.

Part of lesson	Comments/guidance on how to complete
Direct instruction	Here is where I directly tell the students what I want them to learn today. I will model the skill, and involve them as much as possible. I will use multiple examples, and be explicit about how I want them to do things. If there is special language I need to be sure to use, or particular examples I will use, I will write them in this section.
Guided practice	In this part of the lesson, the students will do more practice with the new skill. They might work in pairs, or as a whole (small) group. I will watch them and provide assistance as needed. In this section of the plan, I may write out what I will be looking for as students are working.
Independent practice	Here is where students will practice the skill on their own. This may be for homework, or it may happen in class.
Generalization/ transfer	This may be covered in another part of the lesson. If so, there's no need to say it again! I need to go back through my lesson and see if I've told the students about how they will use this skill in the future. If I haven't told them yet, I will here. I might ask them to tell me where they think they might use the skill. If there is no way this skill will generalize, I will scrap this lesson and plan a different one.
End of the lesson: Preview/review	This is my last chance to talk to the whole class and we can sum up what we did during the lesson. If they have been working alone or in groups up till this point, I will call them all back together. I might ask them if they can tell me what they learned, and/or I might summarize the lesson for them, briefly. I will also tell them what they can look forward to doing the next time we meet.
Data collection (chart that matches the behavioral objective[s])	This is not part of the lesson; this is where I will keep track of whether the students met the behavioral objective. It looks like a chart, with student names on one side, and the objective on the other. Here is a simple example:

	x/20 problems correct	
Mary		
Jim		
Joe		
Sue		

Attach handouts, overheads (not necessarily on acetate), and other materials needed for the lesson to occur.

FIGURE 5.5. *(cont.)*

special education. Therefore, candidates need to have a good grasp of how to help their students become more efficient learners. Knowledge of metacognitive learning strategies is important for candidates to assist their students effectively. To accomplish this goal, special education teacher educators need to be adequately trained to teach these concepts to their candidates, or provide them with access to such training.

Strategies instruction is known under various names, including *Kansas Learning Strategies* or *Strategic Instruction Model* (Deshler & Shumaker, 2006), and *Self-Regulated Strategy Development* (Santangelo, Harris, & Graham, 2007). The basic idea is that the special education teacher is teaching students to learn how to learn, including helping them with memory aids (often mnemonics), attitudes and attributions, goal setting, self-directing through a task or strategy use, self-monitoring performance, and self-reinforcing. Special education teacher educators can also assist candidates in using metacognitive strategies for their own use, especially given the large amount of information they need to master.

For special education teacher educators who may not feel comfortable teaching candidates how to use learning strategies, there are several resources available. One resource which provides step-by-step guidance for candidates (or for teacher educators or other professionals) is the modules developed by the IRIS Center, Peabody College, Vanderbilt University. In the category of Learning Strategies, as of early 2011, there were nine modules, six case studies, and 34 information briefs available. One module in particular which walks through strategy instruction in a methodical way is titled *SRSD: Using Learning Strategies to Enhance Student Learning* (The IRIS Center for Training Enhancements). This module, like many others from IRIS, includes examples, resources, and sound clips and videos from experts and real classrooms, as well as activities to assist students in understanding metacognitive strategy instruction.

Task Analysis

Another important and related skill that special education teachers need, regardless of who their students are, is the ability to task-analyze their students' curriculum. Task analysis has its roots in behavioral theory, and may not appeal for that reason to some candidates or special education teacher educators. However, understanding all the component parts of a task will help candidates know how to approach teaching more effectively. Understanding each detail of a task will assist them in seeing where breakdowns in learning occur, and in knowing how to go back and re-teach particular steps. It can also provide a blueprint for how to approach teaching as well as a model for assessment.

Candidates should learn to task-analyze a wide range of desired student behaviors, both academic and affective. As candidates encounter students who provide challenges to them, the skills of thinking about each step of a task and of being able to sequence them can assist them in teaching their students. Furthermore, understanding and thinking about each step of a student skill or task can help a candidate or teacher spot breakdowns in understanding quickly.

Task analysis can also assist candidates and teachers in communicating with parents. A task analysis is typically written in plain language, and candidates and teachers can share their task analysis with parents and indicate which steps have been mastered, which are currently being worked on, and which have not yet been addressed.

Adaptive Technology

Another area of expertise needed by special education teacher educators is adaptive technology (AT). If an individual faculty member is not up to date in this area, it is crucial that candidates have some way to access this knowledge, and that each faculty member has a working knowledge of the area as it applies to their own situation. AT is a broad term for any type of technology that assists students in learning a skill or area of content that they might otherwise not have access to. The law that addresses this is commonly referred to as The Tech Act. In 1998 the act was renamed the Assistive Technology Act and was reauthorized in 2004. The Tech Act defines AT devices as "any item, piece of equipment, or product system (whether acquired off the shelf, modified, or customized) that is used to increase, maintain, or improve functional capabilities of individuals with disabilities" (*www.nichcy.org/Laws/Other/pages/AssistiveTechnologyAct.aspx*). Examples include a range of aids, from communication boards and toggle switches to calculators, software, and laptops. Currently, and in the foreseeable future, this is an area that is experiencing a huge increase in development of solutions not only for special education students, but for learners in general to handle the explosion of information which individuals in the 21st century will encounter.

How the Brain Works

Additionally, teacher candidates need to have a grasp on how the brain works, including metacognition, plasticity, and more. Not long ago, it was assumed that our brains stopped developing at some point in either our youth or young adulthood. While there is certainly a great deal of growth during one's early years, it has now been discovered that the brain is capable of far more change for far longer in one's life (Begley, 2007). Not only is this good news for all of us, but these recent findings should also encourage special education teachers to stay alert for other developments in brain research which may assist them or their students. More information on this topic is included in Chapter 2.

KEEPING UP

Nearly 15 years ago, Cruickshank (1996) wrote about how teacher educators teach, saying that effective teacher educators combine information with practical experience. Therefore, it is up to each teacher educator to keep up to date on what is happening in the schools, both locally and nationally, and not depend on ever-increasingly distant first-hand knowledge of being a special education teacher. Good special education teacher educators will include case studies, microteaching, minicourses, protocol materials, reflective teaching, and simulations in their instruction.

In the 2005 edition of the report on teacher education from the American Educational Research Association (AERA), Grossman noted several pedagogical approaches and provided critiques of each approach. Little research was noted for many of the approaches, including portfolios, case methods, microteaching, and lab experiences. Video-technology and hypermedia were also deemed athe-oretical. In several of the approaches he noted that candidates could learn specific skills, such as with computer simulation. In sum, more research is needed, and practitioner research (action research) is a reasonable approach. Technology is evolving quickly in the world and in education, so skills that candidates have in designing research and evaluating their practice will serve them well into the future. Further, as teacher educators do research in this under-researched area, we help provide essential skills to candidates by engaging them in research.

Returning to the questions at the beginning of this section, what should we present about common instructional approaches, including those recommended by literature? For teacher educators there is often the dilemma of addressing local practices and helping candidates work within that setting while at the same time letting candidates know which approaches are considered "best practices." Teacher educators need to assist candidates, particularly if they are already teaching, to work within the current system while at the same time working to change it. We are also in the position of debunking myths and questioning faulty practices. Several unsubstantiated practices are still being promoted by some school districts. These include notions of "teaching to learning styles," use of colored overlays, applied kinesiology, and very likely others. Teacher educators need to arm candidates with research-based information to help them make good choices. Additionally, we should help candidates read and interpret research critically.

DO GENERAL EDUCATORS NEED THESE SAME SKILLS?

In her dissertation, Israel (2009) noted that knowledge of the IDEIA and assessment makes special education teacher education different from teacher education in general. Special education is unique in that we are preparing novice special education teachers to differentiate instruction based on individual learning needs and adapting and modifying curricula to meet the needs of individual students. This is a complicated task. The context of systemic problems in the field of special education includes the shortages of special education teachers who are deemed to be "highly qualified" or "highly effective." Should we expect general educators to have these skills as well?

The sections above have described basic knowledge and skills needed to be an effective special educator. However, with increasing inclusion in the schools, as well as the current "highly qualified" or "highly effective" demands on teachers, many special education faculty are being called upon to teach general educators in a much more in-depth way than the typical Introduction to Special Education or Mainstreaming course. Indeed, it can be and has been argued that if special educators need to be experts in the content being taught as well as experts in assessment, identification, accommodations, strategy instruction, behavior change, and other areas, then general educators should be held to similar standards. After all, general educators are also responsible for providing an appropriate education to special education students. Another defensible approach is to require the general educator to be the specialist in content being taught, and the special educator to be the pedagogical expert. As they work together in collaborative, cooperative environments, their shared expertise can bring the best education to all their students, with and without disabilities.

Which interpretation of "highly qualified" or "highly effective" each state adopts will dictate the profile of both the general educators and the special educators in the state. In many cases, practicing general and special education teachers will need to be updated in terms of their skills and expertise to retain their teaching licenses. This can be a big boon to the higher education rolls, but at the same time can fill those classrooms with rather reluctant learners. This poses a challenge to special education (and general education) faculty to make what they are sharing with these learners meaningful. We need to encourage individuals in becoming the best teachers they can be. Approaching staff development opportunities with enthusiasm, and with useful information, will go a long way to improving the field and experiences for all students.

CHAPTER 6

Assessment

Have We Met Our Goals?

Any genuine teaching will result, if successful, in someone's knowing how to bring about a better condition of things than existed earlier.

—John Dewey

To teachers, students are the end products—all else is a means. Hence there is but one interpretation of high standards in teaching: standards are highest where the maximum number of students—slow learners and fast learners alike—develop to their maximal capacity.

—Joseph Seidlin

As good special educators, who now find ourselves in the role of teacher educators, we know that it is important to be able to assess how well our candidates are doing, both along the way and at the end of their preparation. Furthermore, evaluation is a critical component for universities as they undergo program development (Griffin & Pugach, 2007). There are external measures to be sure—PRAXIS II (Educational Testing Service, *www.ets.org*) or some other standardized measure, whether or not our candidates are hired, how well their principals and others find them prepared, whether they stay in the field, their own satisfaction with the profession, and retention data (Zeichner & Conklin, 2005). These are important factors, and programs do need to keep these data. If trends or patterns are noted, adjustments can be made to preparation programs. However, these are factors over which university faculty have less control. Mitigating circumstances such as the state of the economy, the nature of the external measures, and personal choices of candidates may create circumstances where outcome data are difficult to interpret. Preparation programs, then, need to develop assessments that are meaningful for their own circumstances.

Before organizing assessment activities, it is important for stakeholders, usually primarily university faculty, to consider the overall philosophy and goals of the program. This may (and probably should) involve communication and collaboration with general education faculty, as well as consultation with advisory boards. Beck and Kosnik (2006) suggested developing a shared, explicit, philosophy of teaching and learning, in the form of a brief, revisable statement. This statement should be made public in some way, in either written or electronic form. Candidates and potential candidates can be referred to this philosophy and can be invited to make comments and ask questions. The statement should represent integration within and across courses, reflecting the overall orientation of the program. Having candidates develop their own statement as well, revise it at different points in their program, and have a final one for their portfolio can also be useful, not only for the candidate, but as data for program faculty. As programs develop, evolve, and change over time, it is important to intentionally revisit the philosophy to determine if it still reflects the realities of the program. One way to think of this statement is that it is like the United States Constitution—basically unchanging, but revisable—as opposed to the Declaration of Independence—written and signed over 200 years ago and which cannot be changed.

The philosophy of a program should include one overarching or several main goals. Having a goal is critical, even if it's not reached (Guskey, 2000). Just as we teach candidates to create lesson plans that are fluid and subject to change, program plans also should be considered fluid and subject to change. But that doesn't mean you can start out without a plan! We also should be concerned with typical assessment issues of validity, reliability, sampling, use of multiple measures, and timing (Guskey, 2000). In the following paragraphs I offer some considerations, though they should not be taken as a complete list.

Brownell et al. (2003) suggested routine assessments of candidates' learning, based on standards and multiple evidence sources. Many programs choose to have candidates put together a portfolio which demonstrates how they have met various program standards. Some may have some culminating activity in which candidates formally present their evidence. Other programs may just consider success in various courses and student teaching to be sufficient. In most cases, these refer to preparation programs that also culminate in a degree. There are also candidates who are merely seeking certification to teach special education, as they may already hold a degree in something else. These candidates are less likely to be formally assessed, in large part because in many universities these students "don't count" from the university's point of view, since they will not be "degree completers." However, they may be the largest pool of candidates that the university is recommending for licensure. They deserve to be assessed as well. This gives important information to the university program, and should also give important information to these candidates as it does degree-seeking candidates. The process and product of assessment should also give information to faculty and other evaluators. This chapter suggests best practices which should be present in assessments of candidates and programs.

We also obviously need to consider what outcomes we want for new teachers. Since there is little research available (Sindelar et al., 2010), it is likely that programs will remain heterogeneous, at least in the short term. We need to know pedagogical practices that work. As teacher preparation programs are implemented, we (the field) need a variety of data. What is the impact of various pieces of instruction? Does the specific background of teacher educators matter? Is it necessary for the instructor in a methods class to hold a PhD? Or can the courses be delivered better by an excellent master teacher? Research on field experiences indicates (Leko, 2008) that candidates need to be able to apply knowledge from methods classes, otherwise the field experience might serve as a barrier to teacher development (cf. Griffin & Pugach, 2007).

WHO HAS AN INTEREST IN OUR ASSESSMENTS?

When we consider our assessments, we should also consider our audience. Who has an interest in the assessments of our programs? Well, first of all, we do. One of the main purposes of our assessments should be to improve how we are doing our jobs. Did we adequately prepare candidates for the range of students they encounter in their practice? Do they have the tools necessary to assess their students and meet their needs? Do they have the collaborative skills to work with paraprofessionals, general education teachers, administration, and parents? If not, where is the breakdown? What can be changed in our programs to better meet the needs of candidates in the future? As we consider these questions, we might be tempted to make changes to our assessment practices on a near continual basis. However, keep in mind best practices we are teaching our students. When you are trying a new intervention, you need to try it for *long enough* to make a fair assessment about its usefulness. Furthermore, if assessments change along the way, it becomes impossible to make comparisons across time. An assessment plan, agreed upon in advance, can help ensure that programs are evaluated fairly. Often, education changes are referred to as "building a plane while in flight." However, it is possible for special education programs to perhaps build a new plane on the ground while still flying the old one—at least temporarily.

Another important group interested in our assessments is our candidates. They are, of course, interested in the outcome of their individual assessment, but might also be interested in how the special education teacher educator's assessments of each individual compare, and whether and how feedback from the candidates is used. Potential candidates may look to our assessment practices and results when deciding on whether to enlist in a particular program. They are looking for results upon program completion in the form of employability. Potential candidates may want to know about an institution's track record of job placement and employer satisfaction before choosing a particular program.

A third stakeholder with an interest in our assessments is the university in which we do our work. The administration will be interested in numbers of candidates we prepare, and may use this information to defend the existence of a teacher preparation program. Depending on the institution, teacher preparation may not be seen as particularly important, and special education teacher preparation may be poorly understood even within the larger field of education. It is in our own self-preservation interest to articulate clearly and convincingly to administrators why our programs are necessary. For example, the actual numbers of special education candidates may be smaller than other programs, but may in fact be supplying a large proportion of the special education teachers to area schools. Pointing this out to administrators directly can help special education faculty make the case for their value to the community and university. As special education teacher educators, we must be our own best advocates.

Licensing and accrediting bodies are also interested in the assessments of our candidates and programs. In fact, these entities often have a lot of influence on what our programs look like, as our graduates/completers need to meet local licensing requirements. These "outside influences" include state departments of instruction, the U.S. Department of Education, and accrediting bodies such as NCATE (National Council for Accreditation of Teacher Education), TEAC (Teacher Education Accreditation Council), and others. The level of detail each group requires is different, but the questions are similar—are our candidates prepared to enter their classrooms appropriately and fully licensed? These are "surface" requirements, but theoretically imply that deeper competencies, such as those discussed in previous chapters, are in place. As states "sign on to" the newly developed Common Core State Standards (*www.corestandards.org*), preparation programs will need to discover how they impact what is required.

Local school districts are interested in our candidates and how well prepared they are. As noted by Israel (2009), teacher educators as well as schools and colleges of education have a political pressure to address, and remedy, many problems in today's schools. Teacher education programs in universities have come under scrutiny at all levels. In fact, current Secretary of Education Arne Duncan has been a noted critic of teacher education programs in colleges and universities. (e.g., *www2.ed.gov/news/pressreleases/2009/10/10222009a.html*.)

Teacher educators as well as colleges, schools, and departments of education often experience political pressure to remedy many problems in today's public schools (Israel, 2009). We should keep in mind, and be able to argue the points she noted, that schools of education are blamed for social problems not entirely within their scope of influence, including low-performing K–12 schools, and the socioeconomic and cultural achievement gap. The expectation that schools of education respond to all these issues is similar to the general public's expectation that K–12 teachers can provide everything that students need to be successful, regardless of what is going on in their lives outside the school day.

The notion, for example, that all students, regardless of any factors (socio-economic status, disability, prior school experience, facility with English, etc.) will meet grade-level standards on state-normed exams is at its face a ridiculous prospect. However, the current law NCLB has mandated it, and the public expects it. There are some positive aspects to NCLB and the high standards that were set for all students. Accountability for all students' learning is a very good thing. However, NCLB has been commonly referred to as being "all stick and no carrot." The reauthorization of ESEA by the current (112th) Congress may address some of these concerns, but to what extent remains unknown at this point.

Boyd, Lankford, Loeb, and Wyckoff (2005) analyzed choices made by first-year teachers in New York State and found that a majority chose to take their first jobs in their hometowns (61%), or very close to their hometowns (85%). Since teacher education graduates are so likely to return to their hometowns for their teaching careers, school districts where our candidates are from, as well as those located in the vicinity of our programs, are other interested parties. These districts are also more likely to be providing practicum and student teaching placements for us, and therefore want to be assured that these candidates will be an asset to their schools while they are there. Zeichner and Conklin (2005) noted that principal and teacher perceptions of program quality are an important outcome of teacher education programs. Likewise, their ratings of candidate and teacher quality can add information about program quality. Having teachers, administrators, and parents able to provide input to our programs and our assessments will strengthen our programs as well as our relationships with local school districts. Forming advisory boards with these stakeholders and others can provide valuable input to program development efforts.

Finally, the general public has an interest in how well we are preparing candidates, even if they may not be interested in our specific assessment practices. Those who are parents want to know that their children are being taught by individuals who have up-to-date information and are willing and able to help their children achieve everything they possibly can. The public in general is concerned that well-qualified teachers are being produced for the public schools, which they invest in with their tax dollars.

SOURCES OF EVIDENCE

In any good assessment, multiple sources of evidence are important (Blanton et al., 2003; Darling-Hammond, 2006). When assessing outcomes of a single course or course of study, or of an entire program, it is appropriate to seek input from a variety of sources and in a variety of ways. Assessing candidates from a variety of perspectives will help us have a complete picture of whether our goals were met or not. Guskey (2000) suggested the following levels of evaluation for professional development, which apply here as well: (1) organization support and change, (2) participants' reactions, (3) participants' learning, (4) participants' use of new knowledge and skills, and (5) student learning outcomes. These are discussed in the paragraphs that follow.

As we consider organization support and change in light of teacher preparation programs, we make use of various pieces of data and assessment of our candidates. Careful reflection on these will lead to program change over time. As Guskey (2000) noted, this implies a shift in culture, which can take time. Structure can be changed more easily, and doing so can help shift a culture, but effective leadership is required to help the cultural shift occur. Guskey (2000) notes the need for attention to organizational policies and resources, as well as protection from intrusions to the extent possible. He further reminds leaders that they need to foster collegial support and encourage openness to experimentation. Finally, successes must be recognized.

Participants' reactions and learning may be evaluated by student satisfaction surveys. In many cases, these are distributed to candidates at the end of courses. However, individual faculty may want to make these more meaningful by adding items or distributing an additional set of questions. Several excellent ideas can be found in *Classroom Assessment Techniques* (Angelo & Cross, 1993). This book provides techniques for assessing knowledge, skills, and attitudes of candidates and can be used for entire courses or individual assignments of class meetings. Most teacher education programs have a capstone course and/or student teaching, where candidate learning can be more authentically assessed. PRAXIS II (ETS, *www.ets.org*) scores may also provide data about candidate learning.

Participant learning is best assessed through their use of their new knowledge and skills. This can be accomplished through assessments and observations before and after program completion by specifically looking at which knowledge and skills have been learned. In each class, students typically are asked to provide feedback on course satisfaction. Many times these are numerical ratings, and may be conducted on a universitywide basis. However, these may be of little use to faculty. For more meaningful feedback in individual classes, faculty may desire to use a form that provides narrative feedback such as that in Figure 6.1

Of course, we should ultimately be concerned with whether and how candidates use what we have taught. Along the way, as candidates progress through our courses and programs, we can check whether they are using the knowledge and skills we have taught, in both coursework and fieldwork. After candidates complete programs, we can also follow up with principals and other employers to see whether candidates are generalizing this knowledge and these skills. If we offer the best coursework and our candidates exhibit superior performance

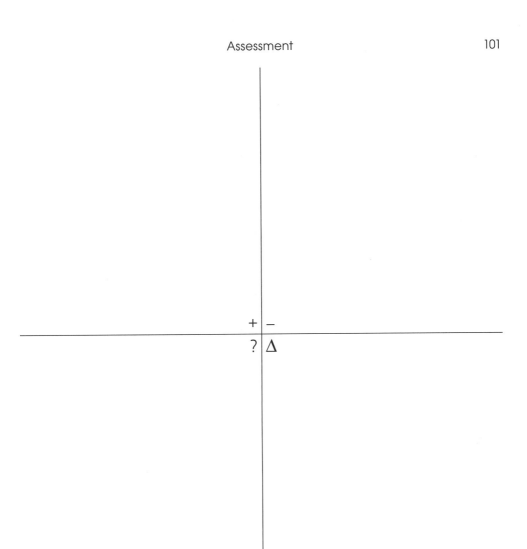

Directions to students: Please use this paper to make note of how things are going for you in class thus far. In the quadrant with a "+" sign, note things that are *positive* from your perspective. In the next quadrant, with a "−" sign, note things which are *negative*. In the lower left quadrant, list any questions you have, and in the lower right quadrant, make comments about any *changes* you would like to see. I will compile all student responses and we will discuss the aggregate results at the next class meeting.

FIGURE 6.1. Simple assessment, to be given during progress of the course.

both along the way and at the end of programs, and yet they do not carry these practices into the classroom, our efforts have been wasted.

Finally, as candidates encounter their own students in their preparation program and after completion, we should be able to assist them in documenting how their students have progressed on their goals. Student progress might be far away from teacher educator control, as there are many intervening factors. However, there should be some positive correlation between our preparation programs and K–12 student learning. After all, it is the education of the student receiving special education services that is our ultimate goal.

Given these levels of evaluation suggested by Guskey (2000), what features of programs should be considered? Darling-Hammond (2006) provided the following list of features to consider in assessments: (1) candidate performance, (2) candidate integration of knowledge/skills in practice, (3) use (or not) of multiple assessment measures, (4) and opportunities for practice. Darling-Hammond's focus was on general education, and did not consider the unique needs of special educators. At any rate, programs designed to train excellent special educators should be able to address each of these in a satisfactory way for all audiences mentioned above. In the following paragraphs, I will suggest ways to address these issues in the context of special education teacher preparation.

Candidate Performance

On-the-ground authentic assessment is the best way to assess most professionals in their jobs. As candidates enter the workforce, they will rarely be afforded opportunities to revise their work or to ask for extensions or other accommodations they are routinely granted in preparation programs. As teacher educators, therefore, we have to strike a balance between giving students multiple opportunities and ways to show us what they know and demanding on-demand, first-time, at- or above-standard performance. Typically, student teaching or another culminating field experience is the place where candidate performance is assessed in an authentic way, and for high stakes. Evaluation of candidates at this point is crucial, and not to be taken lightly. Documentation of progress needs to be thoroughly and carefully done. While it may be appropriate in some cases to consider individual candidate growth, it is important to ensure that the endpoint of each candidate's education is at a high enough level such that all program completers are excellent special education teachers.

Integration of Knowledge and Skills in Practice

Candidates need to be given multiple opportunities to integrate knowledge and skills. Teacher educators need to make explicit where concepts in the lecture hall intersect with practices in the field. A special education teacher candidate should never be in a position to ask "Why are we learning this?" When a field experience assignment is given, candidates should understand the purpose of the assignment, and should have the prerequisite knowledge and skills to complete the assignment. The more grounded all coursework is in the real world of teaching, the deeper the understanding of the candidates.

Multiple Assessment Measures

As discussed earlier, there are many options available for assessment of programs. Guskey (2000) suggested the following ways of assessing teachers' use of new knowledge and skills: (1) direct observations, (2) participant interviews or conferencing, (3) supervisor interviews or conferencing, (4) student interviews or conferencing, (5) questionnaires, (6) focus groups, (7) implementation logs and reflective journals, and (8) participant portfolios. Each of these can be put to use in separate courses or projects, across courses, or in the program as a whole. When assessing candidates, we need to provide multiple opportunities as well. There is value in assessing candidates in individual courses in multiple ways, and assessing candidates in multiple ways throughout the curriculum. As candidates receive instruction from a variety of faculty members, some variation will naturally occur. However, as a program, it is wise to be systematic about how that will happen. As stated at the outset of this chapter, having a basic assessment plan in place will assist in this process.

Opportunities for Practice

As Chapter 3 explains, the more opportunity candidates have to practice in the field with real students in real situations, the deeper the learning will be. Beyond field experiences, though, teacher educators can provide other opportunities for practice of specific skills. Within individual courses, assignments can be developed to provide real or simulated practice with skills. Assessments should describe and evaluate the quality and quantity of these opportunities, and make adjustments to provide better opportunities as needed.

NUTS AND BOLTS

This section addresses how teacher education programs might go about collecting evidence and data for use in assessments. As Guskey (2000) noted, it is important to undertake *deep* evaluation, more than a checklist of "courses taken." In this era of outcomes, competencies, and accountability, state and local school districts are far less concerned with how many classes students have taken. Take, for example, the concepts of classroom management. Employers are not concerned with whether a potential teacher has taken many or even any courses covering the topics of classroom management. They are instead concerned with whether a candidate has the skills to manage a classroom. Therefore, as we evaluate our programs, we need to be critically examining whether our efforts in instructing candidates in classroom management, whether in an entire course or spread across multiple courses, give them the skills they can then translate effectively to classroom practice.

Guskey (2000) considered the program evaluation standards outlined by the Joint Committee on Standards for Educational Evaluation, which fall into four broad categories: utility standards, feasibility standards, proprietary standards, and accuracy standards. Utility standards are intended to ensure evaluations will meet the needs of the users, and include identification of stakeholders and information scope and sequence. Likewise, feasibility standards can help ensure practicality of the evaluations. Proprietary standards include legal and ethical agreements which protect evaluators, those being evaluated, and others affected by results. Finally, accuracy standards relate to the reliability and validity of the evaluations. While these were aimed at school- and district-level professional development and evaluation, they may be applied to teacher preparation programs.

As previously mentioned, many programs assess candidates and programs by the use of portfolios, in which candidates demonstrate whether or not they have met program goals. On the face of it, this is a good practice, but faculty may be hesitant to "fail" a candidate on a particular standard when that candidate had completed that goal in a colleague's course. However, if the portfolio is seen as a formative rather than summative assessment, it can give the faculty an opportunity to see "holes" in their program and give the candidates a chance to refine their offerings. Furthermore, if the expectation is clearly communicated, candidates may be expected to revise and improve final course products before including them in the portfolio.

Another way to think of a portfolio is as a product separate from or in addition to any particular projects in courses. At the very least, if course projects are used, they should be accompanied by a reflection on the part of the candidate about how he/she sees the product contributing to their individual development as a teacher. Wholly separate from course projects, the portfolio could be constructed by the candidate with his/her own evidence about how the standards of the program were addressed. Using portfolios as a program can be of great assistance in program revisions. As candidates submit evidence for evaluation, programs can aggregate data across candidates and across years. Candidate reflections give insight into how well the overarching goals and philosophies of the program have been communicated. When using portfolios, one needs to keep in mind the psychometric properties and instructional utility of assessing candidates in this way (Burns & Haight, 2005; Kossar, 2003).

Assessment data might also include information about candidate satisfaction, both with the program and in their professional life (CEC, 2003, 2009; Zeichner & Conklin, 2005). Measures of job satisfaction might include data about where these new teachers choose to teach upon program completion. Additionally, we need to collect longitudinal data about retention. Are the candidates teaching in situations for which the preparation program provided preparation? Are they seeking additional preparation?

We have the opportunity in special education teacher preparation to assess our programs as a whole, and compare outcomes to other programs. The literature provides information regarding evaluations of the methods of teacher preparation, though it is very sparse, and rarely specific to special education teacher preparation. In comparing 4- or 5-year general education undergraduate programs, the 5-year programs seem to have better results, but Zeichner and Conklin (2005) noted limits in the studies. They also noted variation when considering alternative versus traditional preparation. When the alternative preparation was state sponsored, there were differences depending on subject matter and grade level. Comparisons of district preparation with traditional preparation were inconclusive as well, which may be due to the wide variation in what districts provided in the way of preparation. In the evaluation of candidates who were part of Teach for America, Zeichner and Conklin reported that they felt unprepared. In one state's study (North Carolina), teachers who came from Teach for America had slightly better outcomes than those prepared in traditional university programs. However, these teachers represent a very small percentage of the teaching force, and represent a very select group to begin with.

The ultimate outcome of candidate assessment, of course, is the performance of the candidate's students. Whether or not candidates can affect change in their students is the final test of the success of a teacher preparation program. However, using K–12 student achievement as the only measure of success is not without problems. First of all, special education teachers by definition will have low-achieving students. If student success is measured in a standardized way such as currently required by NCLB, then special education teacher candidates will usually fall behind their general education peers on such measures. Conversely, if success is measured by whether or not IEP goals are met, then there will be too much variability between and among special education teachers to render that a meaningful measure of student growth. Also, success, or not, of K–12 students is dependent on many more variables than the teacher, and teacher performance is dependent on many more variables than the preparation program. Therefore, use of these outcomes is extremely problematic and should be used with great caution. CEC has recommended to Congress the use of indexed measures of achievement which use multiple measures and take variance into account (*www.cec.sped.org*).

Besides variability in our candidates' students, the variability among their work situations can also make determination of success of a program problematic. If, for example, many graduates of a program work in typically high achieving schools, the outcome will look better than for graduates who work in typically low achieving schools, even if the candidates from the latter program are better prepared and have better skills. It shouldn't be a goal of a program to encourage candidates to take jobs in high-achieving areas in order to make the program look good.

ASSESSMENTS DONE "TO" TEACHER EDUCATION

As noted, there are several stakeholders who have an interest in our assessments, from the individual candidates to the public as a whole. Not all will use the same methods, or the same standards, nor do they serve the same purposes. Recently, teacher education programs in colleges and universities have been assessed by the National Council on Teacher Quality (NCTQ), which plans to publish results in late 2012 in *U.S. News & World Report* (USNWR).

As stated by Kate Walsh of the NCTQ, and reinforced by Robert Morse of USNWR, at the 2011 meeting of the American Association of Colleges for Teacher Education (AACTE; *www.vimeo.com/AACTE*), the NCTQ is a conservative organization, with an anti-teacher education bias, created in 2000. Both Walsh and Morse, facing an admittedly unfriendly audience, explained their views on usefulness of the ratings, and why it would be in the best interest of all to respond. In her talk, Ms. Walsh articulated surprise over the anger that had been expressed by the higher education/teacher education community. She stated that the NCTQ had been transparent in their processes, and never hid plans to partner with USNWR. She stated that she had made efforts to move the NCTQ to a more nonpartisan stance. She also explained that it would be in the best interests of institutions of higher education (IHEs) to participate in the data collection. The main reason given for this was that available data would still be collected and ratings would still be made, even in the absence of IHE cooperation.

In her talk, Ms. Walsh criticized the lack of quality and quantity of research in teacher education. However, she also said that despite these shortfalls, there is still a consensus on what is needed in teacher preparation. She noted that school superintendents have reported that they are unhappy with preparation of teachers they hire. On the other hand, in that same panel, Richard Ginsberg of the University of Kansas stated that most graduates of teacher preparation programs are satisfied with their preparation, but are less satisfied with beginning teacher support once they are hired. Given these two stances, from two different viewpoints, it is difficult to assess which view is correct, or if they both have some validity.

Michael Feuer, of George Washington University, noted that teacher education as a whole is not interested in maintaining the status quo, and is perhaps among the most self-reflective and self-evaluative professions. He also pointed out our near obsession as a culture in rating and ranking nearly everything. He then proceeded to "rate the raters" by posing several questions for IHEs to answer to help them decide whether or not to participate in the NCTQ's evaluation. He applauded the various goals stated and implied by the NCTQ and USNWR—to improve teacher education and communicate that to the public. He found the standards to be from good to mediocre in quality. However, the measure themselves and therefore the quality of the inferences were deemed poor. In particular, he found the use of admissions criteria and syllabi problematic.

Richard Ginsberg, from the University of Kansas, followed up with his critique of the NCTQ assessments. He noted that this evaluation has pulled the field together, which is of course quite positive. However, it seems to have done so by providing us with a common enemy. Ginsberg also noted the myriad evaluations we are already participating in, several of which are mentioned elsewhere in this chapter. This assessment by the NCTQ carries with it, according to Dr. Ginsberg, a sense of attack, as if there is an assumption that the field is broken. He called for greater transparency by NCTQ, asking for rubrics that will be used rather than just a list of indicators (available at *www.nctq.org/edschoolreports/national*). He asked questions about the specificity included in the indicators, which implies that there are scientific data behind the statements. For example, there is an indicator that there should be 8 credit hours of math instruction for teacher candidates without explanation of why or how this particular number was chosen. Why not 7? or 9? He questioned whether meeting these standards would result in better teacher preparation. He also questioned whether the published ratings would assist parents or potential candidates in making informed decisions about where to attend college, especially since most teacher education candidates attend school close to where they live.

The most problematic areas of the NCTQ evaluation seem to center around the lack of rubrics, the NCTQ's freedom in making judgments about institutions that don't participate, the focus on inputs such as syllabi, and in general the lack of transparency. Even though Ms. Walsh stated the process has been transparent, that does not mean it is. If stakeholders (IHEs in this case) feel it is not transparent enough, then it isn't. Transparency is a two-way street! Another problem, which was being reported as this book went to press, is that if the NCTQ can't find information, they will declare an institution "failed" in that area. In contrast, the Interstate Teacher Assessment and Support Consortium (InTASC) makes their standards transparent, asks for feedback from professionals in the field, and revises their standards based on that feedback. Particular details of the NCTQ evaluation, like all evaluations, are subject to change, but this example points out the need for teacher educators to be informed about such evaluations.

In studying the NCTQ standards (available at *www.nctq.org/edschoolreports/ national/standardsCompiled.jsp*), they appear to be like many other standards for teacher education, including those laid out in this book. However, there are still several issues. For example, rating programs based on their degree of selectivity appears to be a tautology, and beyond the control of many programs. If we begin in teacher education with stronger candidates, then we are likely to have stronger completers. This helps explain the success of Teach for America, for example. This is an issue similar to the one our graduates have as special educators. If we have the students who, by definition, are not performing as well as their peers, we should not be surprised when they take longer to meet certain standards.

Another question about the NCTQ standards is why some of them do not appear to apply to all areas of teaching. For example, the first three standards under "Grounded Clinical Practice" are (1) Classroom Management, (2) Practice Planning Instruction, and (3) Measurement. These apply just to elementary and secondary programs, but apparently not to special education programs. Likewise, Standard 10, "Struggling Readers," is listed under standards for elementary school teachers, with no indication that it applies to special education!

While there is no way to avoid other people and organizations assessing us as a profession, and publishing those results, we need to stand as a profession ready to help those findings be better understood in the full context of what we do as teacher educators. Special education teacher education may have an even more difficult task, as it may be misunderstood by other parts of teacher education.

In conversations I have had with numerous colleagues on this issue, and about teacher education evaluation in general, there is a consensus that evaluation is a valued and a valuable undertaking. Using the NCTQ assessments as the current example, we are left with several questions, particularly about the conclusions drawn from the data. Like other assessments, NCTQ attempts to draw a straight line from teacher education to teacher development to student achievement. One of the problems, as noted already, is what data they are gathering to determine what is included in "teacher education" (i.e., counting hours of coursework, which texts are used, what is written in syllabi). Another issue is that it is difficult to predict how a teacher will eventually develop—and when they are "fully formed"—how much of that can the teacher preparation program take credit for? Maybe it was their supportive first principal (or second or sixth); maybe it was their supportive spouse. Maybe, it was the teacher preparation program as a whole, or perhaps just one professor, or a fellow candidate. However, there is unlikely to be a uniform answer for each candidate.

NCTQ and other assessments which are similar seem to operate from the assumption that we, as a field, don't have a clear understanding of what teachers need to know in order to be effective. I think we do have at least somewhat of an idea. Isn't that what our programs are based on? The problem is that these vary from place to place, and really are only meant to get candidates to a certain point in development—either beginning teacher or a teacher with a new set of skills we've provided (as in specialty areas). Whether they take what we have offered and run, or take it and wither, or take it and open a popsicle stand, does not necessarily mean that what we have provided was or was not valuable.

Trying to draw a straight line from my class of candidates to their class of students is impossible. There are way too many intervening variables! But that won't stop the outside evaluators from trying. So the question then is—how can we point out those variables without making them seem like excuses?

CONCLUSION

In general, we should not hesitate in special education teacher education, or in teacher education in general, to take our future into our own hands, and come up with reasonable and defensible evaluations, and publish them for the general public. At present, teacher education is in a reactionary mode to the NCTQ evaluation. These issues should be addressed. Hopefully, though, we can work together as a field to move forward.

Assessment of our candidates and our programs needs to be approached carefully. Like any assessment, error is to be expected and needs to be taken into account. However, with multiple measures and assessments across time we can minimize this error. Guskey (2000) gave the following guidelines for evaluation of professional development, which can apply to the evaluation of teacher education programs. Using these guidelines, which were addressed in this chapter, programs can conduct meaningful evaluations: (1) clarify intended goals, (2) assess value of goals, (3) analyze the content, (4) estimate program's potential to meet goals, (5) determine how goals can be assessed, (6) outline strategies for gathering evidence, and (7) gather and analyze all of above. While these procedures seem obvious to many special educators, who commonly assess and interpret assessments of special education students, applying these procedures to candidate performance might not seem as straightforward. Teacher educators have to keep in mind the multiple audiences for these assessments, and attempt to provide information that will be meaningful and helpful to them. The primary stakeholder, the candidate, should be able to use the assessments to inform their practice to become excellent special educators.

CHAPTER 7

Preparing Excellent Special Educators

Nobody starts out as a completely effective and creative teacher. . . .
The desire to teach and the ability to teach well are not the same
thing. With the rarest of exceptions, one has to learn how to become
a good teacher.

—HERBERT KOHL

In this book, I have attempted to provide an outline of what we can currently
consider to be "best practice" in special education teacher preparation. I have
done so with a bit of trepidation, as the state of education and information available seems to be changing daily. Since I began writing, we elected Barack Obama
as President of the United States, in large part by his promise of "change." That
is an easy promise to keep, since nothing is certain except change! Some of the
changes we can look for in the next several years in education have to do with the
reauthorization of two of our most important laws influencing education: ESEA
(NCLB) and IDEIA. The Higher Education Act was also reauthorized in 2008.

However, some ideas about teacher education are timeless. We are still interested, as special education teacher educators, in designing effective preparation
programs, and still determine effectiveness, in large part, by "generating a relatively permanent change in the behaviors" of our candidates (Thiagarajan et al.,
1974, p. 4). We still have schools which since 1975 have sought to educate everyone, and the variance of student abilities has always existed. Teachers are still

needed to address these students' needs, and they come to us, as teacher educators, to gain the knowledge and skills they must have to do this. Candidates will still have to understand their students, know how to work within the realities of the school systems, and understand the requirements of the laws that govern their practices. As much as things are certainly changing, we still have, in special education teacher education, a critically important role to play in making sure that the next generation of special educators is equipped to face the future with their students.

As we continue to provide an appropriate education for all learners, the field of special education will continue to run up against several dilemmas. They will be addressed differently depending on the overall emphases in K–12 education, as well as teacher education and higher education in general. Some of these perennial dilemmas include: What counts for "content knowledge" of special education teachers? Should special education teachers be generally prepared across categorical areas or more specially prepared? Should special education students be held to the same standards as general education students? Should special education teachers come from the ranks of general education teachers or be dually prepared in general education and special education? Or, is it sufficient to be prepared in special education alone?

In general education teacher education, it is common to find programs with a well-articulated theory that underlies courses, field experiences, and so on. In special education teacher education, however, Brownell and colleagues (2003) noted that this was not as likely. Special education programs might draw from multiple orientations. This might not be a problem if the orientation is clearly articulated and there is appropriate buy-in from all stakeholders. The theoretical orientation a program chooses should be based on available research about teaching, learning, teacher education, and disabilities, at the very least.

IMPORTANT ACTIVITIES IN TEACHER EDUCATION

Beck and Kosnik (2006) presented a host of activities for teacher education programs which go beyond coursework and fieldwork and help induct candidates into the profession. They suggested orientation activities, social activities, and use of electronic communication, which help to create and maintain a sense of program history and identity. They suggest modeling community in faculty teams, and in caring for student teachers. Beck and Kosnik also noted challenges to accomplishing these goals, which include challenges of workload, intensity of program, complexity of relationships, university pressure to increase enrollment, and faculty and student skepticism. Additional challenges they noted were demanding students, finding suitable schools and mentors, and shortage of program time, especially in the current climate. Some of these will continue to be challenges, and are simply inherent to the task of educating teachers. Some

My Personal Journey in Disability Awareness

I have always had people with disabilities in my life. Initially, they were the students my mother taught when she provided home-bound instruction for students in Danville, VA. This was in the late 1960s, and most of her students had cerebral palsy to the extent that it affected their ability to get around without a wheelchair. Back then, of course, they could be turned away from enrolling in their local schools, and it is to the school district's credit that they hired my mother to provide something for these children. She would take me with her on many of these trips to teach, and I would either "help her" teach, or would be sent to go play outside if it was a nice day. I much preferred helping her, though. Those early experiences modeled an incredible amount of patience, and especially the creative problem solving that was required on my mother's part. Many of her students were nonverbal, and I remember even then her saying that she didn't know what her students knew since they couldn't tell her. She played a lot of "20 questions" with them, and was able to teach basic reading and math to them.

Later on, I observed and helped in my mother's special education classes in Indianapolis, where she taught in a separate public school for students with moderate to profound intellectual disabilities. These were in the years just following the passage of the federal special education law; since then that school closed and the students and teachers were sent to neighborhood-based schools. At that school, though, which is also where I did my student teaching, my mother led a Girl Scout troop, and she coached the boys' Special Olympics basketball team all the way to the State Championship! Again, in watching her, and in working in that school with the other teachers, I learned so much about what it meant to treat people with dignity and care.

Fast forward to about 20 years later. I have been a special education teacher in three different states, have gotten a master's degree and a PhD in special education, and am starting my first job in higher education. Suddenly (or at least I wasn't expecting it), a close family member checked himself into a hospital for severe depression. Up until then, I had always been able to "go home" after a heroic day of working with other people's children. Now, it is up close and personal. To protect identity, I will just list a few things I learned from this experience:

1. Family members and other important caregivers need to be listened to more than they are.
2. People with disabilities often know what they need more than the "experts" do.
3. Professionals—well-meaning, good ones—have a tendency to use jargon when talking to people outside their field.
4. The health care system in our country is badly broken.
5. If the only tool you have is a hammer, everything looks like a nail. In my experience, there were a variety of professionals involved. The psychiatrists wanted to prescribe medicine, the social worker wanted the home life to be safe and stable, the psychologist wanted to know about how he was "feeling" about everything. In this particular case, none of them was that good at talking to the others to come up with a good coordinated plan.
6. There is still a huge stigma around mental illness, which makes getting better that much more difficult.

(cont.)

Just a few years after this had occurred, I got another view of what disability means. In late 1996, just a few weeks after getting married, I noticed that I had lost feeling in one of my arms. Like many busy workaholics, I assumed it would go away, or that I had carpal tunnel syndrome or something like that. It did not go away and in fact spread to various parts of my body. My primary care doctor sent me to a physical therapist, thinking that it was some sort of pinched nerve in my spine, or something else structural. Several specialists, and a couple of MRIs, later, I was diagnosed with multiple sclerosis. Luckily, so far, it has been fairly benign, though the first 5 or more years I did have issues with mobility in that I couldn't walk long distances, and worse for me, couldn't dance without my legs going numb.

From this experience, actually *having* a disability, I have gained even more empathy for others who have disabilities. The experiences with the "experts" have also been interesting. I was lucky to find a neurologist who would treat me as an individual, rather than a "patient with MS." Therefore, I have been able to remain off any drug therapies at this point, and currently am enjoying a pretty symptom-free life. However, I do in fact have this disability, and I know that things could change. I don't know that it alters any day-to-day decisions I make, but I do know how important it is for individuals who have disabilities to learn to advocate for themselves.

As a teacher educator, I use all these experiences to help candidates come to understand issues of disability and to hopefully increase their awareness and sensitivity to individual situations. I also find myself listening to my candidates a lot more closely than I might otherwise have done. Many of us in special education have similar stories to tell, and to think about, as we educate the next generation of teachers. By opening up about our own experiences, we can also learn from others by encouraging them to tell their stories.

require further study and research. Others I have attempted to address in this book.

As noted in the first chapter, quality teacher preparation includes these following six dimensions from *No Dream Denied* (National Commission on Teaching and America's Future, 2003):

1. Careful recruitment and selection of teacher candidates.
2. Strong academic preparation for teaching, including deep knowledge of subjects and a firm understanding of how students learn.
3. Extensive clinical practice to develop effective teaching skills, including an ability to teach specific content effectively, at specific grade levels, to diverse students.
4. Entry-level teaching support through residencies and mentored induction.
5. Modern learning technologies that are imbedded in academic preparation, clinical practice, induction, and ongoing professional development.
6. Assessment of teacher preparation program effectiveness.

Issues with the Research

As noted previously, special education teacher preparation has a weak research base, as does teacher preparation in general. This weak foundation makes it an easy target for critics. Sindelar et al. (2010) focused on high-incidence disabilities in their review of the state of special education teacher education research. Clearly this is an area wide open with research possibilities. Much of the current available research has been conducted about general education teacher education practices. If special education is a separate field, it needs to be more proactive in defining itself as a unique entity, and special education teacher educators need to establish lines of research regarding teacher preparation.

According to research conducted in Florida, special education teacher preparation does matter for higher achievement of students with disabilities (Feng, Figlio, & Sass, 2010; Sindelar et al., 2010). Unfortunately, there is not yet a literature base as to which elements of preparation, or which field experience contexts are essential. Given that there is so much variation within and between states, it may be difficult to discover conclusive national data. Some confounding variables include the different methods of and routes to teacher licensure, the teaching practices in the schools, and the demographics of each state. Conclusions can be made on a state-by-state basis, though, and that data should be available to teacher education programs.

Grossman (2005) noted other issues with teacher preparation research, including needing to carefully define context, and making methods explicit. Since much teacher education research is essentially self-study, there needs to be well-articulated theory and attention to outcomes. Brownell, Bishop, and Sindelar (2004) reminded us that we can be sure that teachers make a difference, and that high-quality teachers are better. When conducting teacher quality research in special education, though, we must address the current policy context which values student outcomes and questions teacher preparation. Their research had the goal of describing what effective beginning teacher practice looks like, using student engagement as the dependent variable. They discovered, not surprisingly, that beginning teachers have struggles promoting student engagement. Therefore, we should provide candidates with pedagogy that promotes rather than regulates participation and assist them to be responsive to student learning and understanding. We can help candidates to provide cohesive, well-coordinated lessons and create a safe and supportive environment for student participation. However, clearly beginning teachers need ongoing learning on the job, so we should seek to foster an attitude of life-long learning.

Finally, Darling-Hammond (2006) reminds us that a transmission teaching model is no longer adequate for today's learners, if it ever was. Teacher educators need to keep in mind that candidates come to our classrooms with prior knowledge and their students do as well. We need to help candidates organize and use knowledge conceptually in order to apply it beyond the university classroom.

Clearly, preparing special education teachers is a complex job. Those of us who have taken on this task have an enormous, and difficult, responsibility. In one respect, we cannot foresee what our candidates will face as they launch their careers. My hope, and my suspicion, is that the knowledge base will continue to expand, and resources will continue to be made available, so that their jobs might be made easier in some respects. However, I am equally suspicious that their jobs may be more complicated. By providing an excellent foundation for them, and by modeling and promoting an attitude of life-long learning, they will be excellent ambassadors for us to the future.

List of Abbreviations

AT   assistive technology

AACTE   American Association of Colleges for Teacher Education (*aacte.org*)

ATE   Association of Teacher Educators (*www.ate1.org*)

CEC   Council for Exceptional Children (*www.cec.sped.org*)

CLD   culturally and linguistically diverse

COPPSE   Center on Personnel Studies in Special Education

ELLs   English language learners

ESEA   Elementary and Secondary Education Act (*ed.gov*)

ETS   Educational Testing Service

FAPE   free and appropriate public education

IDEIA   Individuals with Disabilities Education Improvement Act of 2004

IEP   individualized education plan or program

IHE   Institution of Higher Education

InTASC	Interstate Teacher Assessment and Support Consortium
K–12	kindergarten through 12th grade
LEA	local education agency
LRE	least restrictive environment
NBPTS	National Board of Professional Teaching Standards
NCATE	National Council for Accreditation of Teacher Education
NCLB	No Child Left Behind
NCTQ	National Council on Teacher Quality
OSEP	Office of Special Education Programs
PBIS	positive behavior interventions and supports
RTI	response to intervention
SEA	state education agency
SPeNSE	Study of Personnel Needs in Special Education
TEAC	Teacher Education Accreditation Council
TED	Teacher Education Division (of CEC)
USNWR	*U.S. News & World Report*

Annotated Bibliography

Beck, C., & Kosnik, C. (2006). *Innovations in teacher education: A social constructivist approach.* Albany, NY: SUNY Press.

In this book, Beck and Kosnik explain social constructivism, and how this framework is useful in preservice teacher education. This could be useful for programs that are interested in learning about social constructivism, and are looking for models to use. The authors provide examples of how to create an integrated program with university and K–12 school partnerships. All of their examples are from general education programs, but their ideas are still useful for special education. They include a substantial discussion of practicum sites—how to choose them, various issues involved, and how they should be integrated into university coursework. They also include examples of programs and their philosophy statements.

Billingsley, B. S. (2005). *Cultivating and keeping committed special education teachers: What principals and district leaders can do.* Thousand Oaks, CA: Corwin Press.

The retention of special education teachers is a big issue for anyone invested in the field, but probably especially for principals and others in school districts who find themselves in the position of hiring and providing support to special education teachers. In this book, Dr. Billingsley provides ideas for those stakeholders so that their special education positions are not continually being filled by new hires. The sections of the book include (1) understanding teacher attrition and retention, (2) finding and cultivating high-quality special educators, and (3) creating positive work environments. Every aspect of employing special educators is considered here, and readers are encouraged to consider the "whole teacher," just as we expect teachers to consider the "whole child."

Cochran-Smith, M., & Zeichner, K. M. (Eds.). (2005). *Studying teacher education: The report of the AERA panel on research and teacher education.* Mahwah, NJ: Erlbaum.

This volume provides a comprehensive view of the status of teacher education research. Several areas of research are covered: teacher demographics, indicators of teacher quality, effects of coursework in arts and science and foundations of education, methods courses and field experiences, pedagocial approaches, preparing teachers for diverse populations, preparing teachers to work with students with disabilities, account-ability in teacher education, and teacher education programs. Chapter 9, *Research on Pre-paring General Education Teachers to Work with Students with Disabilities,* is probably of most interest to readers of this book. It was written by Marleen Pugach, and reviews literature on what is known about preparing general education teachers to work with special edu-cation students. This would be a useful chapter for readers who are involved in providing such instruction to general education candidates, which, as Dr. Pugach points out, is part of most general education preparation programs. Aside from this chapter, the volume is more concerned with general education preparation, or general teacher education issues that may have applicability to special education programs as well.

Council for Exceptional Children. (2009). *What every special educator must know: Ethics, standards, and guidelines* (6th ed., rev.). Arlington, VA: Author.

This is commonly referred to as "The Red Book," and is an indispensible resource for anyone involved in preparing special education teachers. Many preparation programs as well as states derive their standards for teachers, paraprofessionals, and others from the standards in this book. The standards contained therein are constantly under discussion and revision, so teacher educators who wish to assure that they are most up-to-date are referred to the CEC website (*www.cec.sped.org*).

Darling-Hammond, L. (2006). *Powerful teacher education: Lessons from exemplary programs.* San Francisco: Jossey-Bass.

This book reports a major study by Darling-Hammond, and describes seven exem-plary teacher preparation programs. The seven programs were chosen from a national reputational survey, as well as other surveys of principals, beginning teachers, and teach-ers who were graduates of the identified programs. Her research team also conducted observations of the graduates in their early years of classroom teaching. Thus, what is presented in this book includes rich description and grounded conclusions about what should be included in teacher education programs. The programs described in the book are all geared toward preparing general education teachers, and only a brief part of one chapter is about preparing those teachers to teach students with disabilities. However, the general guidelines and findings from this study are robust, and can be extrapolated to special education programs.

Darling-Hammond, L., & Baratz-Snowden, J. (Eds.). (2005). *A good teacher in every classroom: Preparing the highly qualified teachers our children deserve.* San Francisco: Jossey-Bass.

This brief report is based on a larger volume, and is sponsored by the National Acad-emy of Education. The goals of this report are to present what beginning teachers need to know, to describe best practices for helping them acquire that knowledge, and to suggest policies needed to assure that new teachers can adequately serve their students from the first day. It is focused on general education, and in fact has only a little more than two pages out of 83 that address teaching diverse learners. However, the general guidance, including what good teachers need to know and how to help them acquire those skills and knowledge, can be applied to all areas of education.

Duffy, M. L., & Forgan, J. (2005). *Mentoring new special education teachers: A guide for mentors and program developers*. Thousand Oaks, CA: Corwin Press.

This book is targeted toward school district personnel who are interested in providing mentors and general personnel development for special educators. Extensive information about how to develop a mentoring program is the focus of the book. The first part of the book helps readers understand some of the characteristics of new special education teachers. Then, how to select mentors and help them develop good communication skills is included. This section includes possible barriers that may be encountered, and how to listen and observe. The book contains several charts, tables, and ideas, which can be put to practical use. The information might also be useful to university faculty who are supervising student teachers or practicum students.

Guskey, T. R. (2000). *Evaluating professional development*. Thousand Oaks, CA: Corwin Press.

Professional development is provided with regularity in school districts and other places where continual refining of skills is required. However, as the author of this text points out, without evaluating these efforts, we cannot know whether the professional development has been effective. While this text is geared toward school systems and other providers of professional development to LEAs, there are applications to teacher educators. Teacher education as a whole can be thought of as prolonged professional development, and graduate programs in particular are more directly professional development. The text begins with definitions of both professional development and evaluation, and why each is important. Five levels of evaluation are then described: (1) participants' reactions, (2) participants' learning, (3) organization and support change, (4) participants' use of new knowledge and skills, and (5) student learning outcomes. The final chapter is about how to present evaluation results. Many of the ideas presented in this text are summarized in Chapter 6. This text is recommended especially for teacher educators who are preparing to undergo major evaluation and/or revision efforts.

Guyton, E. M., & Dangel, J. R. (Eds.). (2004). *Research linking teacher preparation and student performance: Teacher education yearbook XII*. Dubuque, IA: Kendall-Hunt.

In this yearbook from the ATE, the editors assembled research that addressed the linkages between teacher (candidate) preparation and student (K–12) performance. The issues in making these connections are explored, and various models for assessing teacher impact are described. The 11 chapters are divided into three sections: 1. Effects of teacher education interventions in student learning. 2. Methods of making connections between teacher education and student learning. 3. Models for assessing teacher impact on student learning. While the focus of this volume is general education, those interested in pursuing research in special education teacher preparation and its linkages to student learning can find models here. In the overview of the book, Alan Reiman describes the gaps in our understanding of teacher professional development. First, he notes that teacher education tends to be relatively brief and episodic. Secondly, we don't adequately understand the relationship between teacher thinking and student learning. Finally, only a few professional development interventions have detectable effects on classroom instruction and student learning. Furthermore, these effects are rarely lasting. Clearly more research is needed, particularly since teacher education programs are routinely evaluated on demonstrating these linkages.

McLaughlin, M. J., & Nolet, V. (2004). *What every principal needs to know about special education*. Thousand Oaks, CA: Corwin Press.

This book describes, from the point of view of two special education teacher educators, five principles that are essential for every school principal to know and understand, and be able to implement in their schools. These five principles are: 1. Understanding the legal basis for special education; 2. Understanding that effective special education involves matching instruction to learner needs, not to disability label; 3. Understanding that special education is neither a place nor a program, but a set of services; 4. Understanding how to include all students in assessments; and 5. Understanding how to create supportive schoolwide conditions. These five principles are discussed from the standpoint of special education teachers' needs and special education teacher educators' roles. The book expands on each of these ideas in three sections, with key ideas at the beginning of each section. This book is recommended for special education teacher educators who have the opportunity to teach in MSA programs. It would also be helpful for special education teachers who have to assist their principals, who may have limited knowledge of special education.

Sullivan, S., & Glanz, J. (2009). *Supervision that improves teaching and learning: Strategies and techniques* (3rd ed.). Thousand Oaks, CA: Corwin Press.

This book is targeted toward principals and others who find themselves in the position of supervising and providing support to practicing teachers. It is written as a text for those in graduate programs to become principals, and thus contains case studies and other problems for readers to consider. Three interpersonal approaches to supervision are described: direct informational, collaborative, and self-directed. Several observation tools are included, which may be of use to special education teacher educators in their role as field supervisor. The clinical supervision cycle as well as other supervisory approaches is described in part in Chapter 4 of this volume, but those who seek further details, and possible forms to use, are directed to this text. The thrust of this text, rather than being purely evaluative or punitive, is the use of supervision for the growth of teaching practices.

Thiagarajan, S., Semmel, D. S., & Semmel, M. I. (1974). *Instructional development for training teachers of exceptional children: A sourcebook*. Reston, VA: Council for Exceptional Children.

This was one of the first if not the first book to describe how programs for teacher preparation in special education might be developed. Maynard Reynolds noted in the foreword that although the material focuses on "special education, this work can be used productively in other fields that lack sufficient or adequate instructional tools." While its usefulness for special education and other fields has been touted, it sadly represents the last effort to describe special education teacher development in a comprehensive way. The book was a joint publication of two university centers (University of Minnesota and Indiana University), the CEC, and the Teacher Education Division of the CEC. As someone who received her first special education teacher training from Indiana University in the 1970s, I can attest to familiarity with the approaches described. Heavy emphasis is placed on task analysis, not just for use in teaching special education students, but as a task analysis of the job of teaching also. This gave special education teacher educators a reference point for how to instruct candidates.

Vallecorsa, A. L., deBettencourt, L. U., & Garriss, E. (1992). *Special education programs: A guide to evaluation.* Newbury Park, CA: Corwin Press.

This brief volume covers several areas that can be used by school programs for the evaluation of special education programs. It is meant to be used by practitioners rather than professional evaluators, and thus has specific suggestions which are user friendly. The handbook is dated, but the information is still useful. Issues covered include: teacher needs for staff development, appropriateness of LRE placements, and satisfaction of program participants. Additionally, evaluation materials are provided to help document what is going on in classrooms, as well as what is in IEPs. The final section covers the generalization of student skills to other settings.

Council for Exceptional Children Standards for Professional Practice

STANDARD 1: FOUNDATIONS

Special educators understand the field as an evolving and changing discipline based on philosophies, evidence-based principles and theories, relevant laws and policies, diverse and historical points of view, and human issues that have historically influenced and continue to influence the field of special education and the education and treatment of individuals with exceptional needs both in school and society. Special educators understand how these influence professional practice, including assessment, instructional planning, implementation, and program evaluation. Special educators understand how issues of human diversity can impact families, cultures, and schools, and how these complex human issues can interact with issues in the delivery of special education services. They understand the relationships of organizations of special education to the organizations and functions of schools, school systems, and other agencies. Special educators use this knowledge as a ground upon which to construct their own personal understandings and philosophies of special education.

Beginning special educators demonstrate their mastery of this standard through the mastery of the CEC Common Core Knowledge and Skills, as well as through the appropriate CEC Specialty Area(s) Knowledge and Skills for which the program is preparing candidates.

STANDARD 2: DEVELOPMENT AND CHARACTERISTICS OF LEARNERS

Special educators know and demonstrate respect for their students first as unique human beings. Special educators understand the similarities and differences in human development and the characteristics between and among individuals with and without exceptional learning needs. Moreover, special educators understand how exceptional conditions can interact with the domains of human development and they use this knowledge to respond to the varying abilities and behaviors of individuals with exceptional learning needs. Special educators understand how the experiences of individuals with exceptional learning needs can impact families, as well as the individual's ability to learn, interact socially, and live as fulfilled contributing members of the community.

Beginning special educators demonstrate their mastery of this standard through the mastery of the CEC Common Core Knowledge and Skills, as well as through the appropriate CEC Specialty Area(s) Knowledge and Skills for which the preparation program is preparing candidates.

STANDARD 3: INDIVIDUAL LEARNING DIFFERENCES

Special educators understand the effects that an exceptional condition can have on an individual's learning in school and throughout life. Special educators understand that the beliefs, traditions, and values across and within cultures can affect relationships among and between students, their families, and the school community. Moreover, special educators are active and resourceful in seeking to understand how primary language, culture, and familial backgrounds interact with the individual's exceptional condition to impact the individual's academic and social abilities, attitudes, values, interests, and career options. The understanding of these learning differences and their possible interactions provides the foundation upon which special educators individualize instruction to provide meaningful and challenging learning for individuals with exceptional learning needs.

Beginning special educators demonstrate their mastery of this standard through the mastery of the CEC Common Core Knowledge and Skills, as well as through the appropriate CEC Specialty Area(s) Knowledge and Skills for which the program is preparing candidates.

STANDARD 4: INSTRUCTIONAL STRATEGIES

Special educators posses a repertoire of evidence-based instructional strategies to individualize instruction for individuals with exceptional learning needs. Special educators select, adapt, and use these instructional strategies to promote challenging learning results in general and special curricula and to appropriately modify learning environments for individuals with exceptional learning needs. They enhance the learning of critical thinking, problem solving, and performance skills of individuals with exceptional learning needs, and increase their self-awareness, self-management, self-control, self-reliance, and self-esteem. Moreover, special educators emphasize the development, maintenance, and generalization of knowledge and skills across environments, settings, and the lifespan.

Beginning special educators demonstrate their mastery this standard through the mastery of the CEC Common Core Knowledge and Skills, as well as through the appropriate CEC Specialty Area(s) Knowledge and Skills for which the program is preparing candidates.

STANDARD 5: LEARNING ENVIRONMENTS AND SOCIAL INTERACTIONS

Special educators actively create learning environments for individuals with exceptional learning needs that foster cultural understanding, safety and emotional well-being, positive social interactions, and active engagement of individuals with exceptional learning needs. In addition, special educators foster environments in which diversity is valued and individuals are taught to live harmoniously and productively in a culturally diverse world. Special educators shape environments to encourage the independence, self-motivation, self-direction, personal empowerment, and self-advocacy of individuals with exceptional learning needs. Special educators help their general education colleagues integrate individuals with exceptional learning needs in regular environments and engage them in meaningful learning activities and interactions. Special educators use direct motivational and instructional interventions with individuals with exceptional learning needs to teach them to respond effectively to current expectations. When necessary, special educators can safely intervene with individuals with exceptional learning needs in crisis. Special educators coordinate all these efforts and provide guidance and direction to paraeducators and others, such as classroom volunteers and tutors.

Beginning special educators demonstrate their mastery of this standard through the mastery of the CEC Common Core Knowledge and Skills, as well as through the appropriate CEC Specialty Area(s) Knowledge and Skills for which the preparation program is preparing candidates.

STANDARD 6: LANGUAGE

Special educators understand typical and atypical language development and the ways in which exceptional conditions can interact with an individual's experience with and use of language. Special educators use individualized strategies to enhance language development and teach communication skills to individuals with exceptional learning needs. Special educators are familiar with augmentative, alternative, and assistive technologies to support and enhance communication of individuals with exceptional needs. Special educators match their communication methods to an individual's language proficiency and cultural and linguistic differences. Special educators provide effective language models, and they use communication strategies and resources to facilitate understanding of subject matter for individuals with exceptional learning needs whose primary language is not English.

Beginning special educators demonstrate their mastery of language for and with individuals with exceptional learning needs through the mastery of the CEC Common

Core Knowledge and Skills, as well as through the appropriate CEC Specialty Area(s) Knowledge and Skills for which the preparation program is preparing candidates.

STANDARD 7: INSTRUCTIONAL PLANNING

Individualized decision-making and instruction is at the center of special education practice. Special educators develop long-range individualized instructional plans anchored in both general and special curricula. In addition, special educators systematically translate these individualized plans into carefully selected shorter-range goals and objectives taking into consideration an individual's abilities and needs, the learning environment, and a myriad of cultural and linguistic factors. Individualized instructional plans emphasize explicit modeling and efficient guided practice to assure acquisition and fluency through maintenance and generalization. Understanding of these factors as well as the implications of an individual's exceptional condition, guides the special educator's selection, adaptation, and creation of materials, and the use of powerful instructional variables. Instructional plans are modified based on ongoing analysis of the individual's learning progress. Moreover, special educators facilitate this instructional planning in a collaborative context including the individuals with exceptionalities, families, professional colleagues, and personnel from other agencies as appropriate. Special educators also develop a variety of individualized transition plans, such as transitions from preschool to elementary school and from secondary settings to a variety of postsecondary work and learning contexts. Special educators are comfortable using appropriate technologies to support instructional planning and individualized instruction.

Beginning special educators demonstrate their mastery of this standard through the mastery of the CEC Common Core Knowledge and Skills, as well as through the appropriate CEC Specialty Area(s) Knowledge and Skills for which the preparation program is preparing candidates.

STANDARD 8: ASSESSMENT

Assessment is integral to the decision-making and teaching of special educators and special educators use multiple types of assessment information for a variety of educational decisions. Special educators use the results of assessments to help identify exceptional learning needs and to develop and implement individualized instructional programs, as well as to adjust instruction in response to ongoing learning progress. Special educators understand the legal policies and ethical principles of measurement and assessment related to referral, eligibility, program planning, instruction, and placement for individuals with exceptional learning needs, including those from culturally and linguistically diverse backgrounds. Special educators understand measurement theory and practices for addressing issues of validity, reliability, norms, bias, and interpretation of assessment results. In addition, special educators understand the appropriate use and limitations of various types of assessments. Special educators collaborate with families and other colleagues to assure nonbiased, meaningful assessments and decision-making. Special educators conduct formal and informal assessments of behavior, learning, achievement, and environments to design learning experiences that support the growth and development of individuals with exceptional learning needs. Special educators use assessment information to identify supports and adaptations required for individuals with exceptional learning needs to access the general curriculum and to participate in school, system, and statewide assessment programs. Special educators regularly monitor the progress of individuals with exceptional learning needs in general and special curricula. Special educators use appropriate technologies to support their assessments.

Beginning special educators demonstrate their mastery of this standard through the mastery of the CEC Common Core Knowledge and Skills, as well as through the appropriate CEC Specialty Area(s) Knowledge and Skills for which the preparation program is preparing candidates.

STANDARD 9: PROFESSIONAL AND ETHICAL PRACTICE

Special educators are guided by the profession's ethical and professional practice standards. Special educators practice in multiple roles and complex situations across wide age and developmental ranges. Their practice requires ongoing attention to legal matters along with serious professional and ethical considerations. Special educators engage in professional activities and participate in learning communities that benefit individuals with exceptional learning needs, their families, colleagues, and their own professional growth. Special educators view themselves as lifelong learners and regularly reflect on and adjust their practice. Special educators are aware of how their own and others attitudes, behaviors, and ways of communicating can influence their practice. Special educators understand that culture and language can interact with exceptionalities, and are sensitive to the many aspects of diversity of individuals with exceptional learning needs and their families. Special educators actively plan and engage in activities that foster their professional growth and keep them current with evidence-based best practices. Special educators know their own limits of practice and practice within them.

Beginning special educators demonstrate their mastery of this standard through the mastery of the CEC Common Core Knowledge and Skills, as well as through the appropriate CEC Specialty Area(s) Knowledge and Skills for which the preparation program is preparing candidates.

STANDARD 10: COLLABORATION

Special educators routinely and effectively collaborate with families, other educators, related service providers, and personnel from community agencies in culturally responsive ways. This collaboration assures that the needs of individuals with exceptional learning needs are addressed throughout schooling. Moreover, special educators embrace their special role as advocate for individuals with exceptional learning needs. Special educators promote and advocate the learning and well-being of individuals with exceptional learning needs across a wide range of settings and a range of different learning experiences. Special educators are viewed as specialists by a myriad of people who actively seek their collaboration to effectively include and teach individuals with exceptional learning needs. Special educators are a resource to their colleagues in understanding the laws and policies relevant to Individuals with exceptional learning needs. Special educators use collaboration to facilitate the successful transitions of individuals with exceptional learning needs across settings and services.

Beginning special educators demonstrate their mastery of this standard through the mastery of the CEC Common Core Knowledge and Skills, as well as through the appropriate CEC Specialty Area(s) Knowledge and Skills for which the preparation program is preparing candidates.

Council for Exceptional Children
Personnel Preparation Standards

a. Programs preparing individuals for entry level or advanced special education professional roles shall adhere to CEC professional standards, by seeking CEC official recognition through the evidence-based process of program review.

b. Program review includes examination of evidence to document quality practice in:

(1) Conceptual Framework Programs have a conceptual framework that establishes the program vision and its relationship to the program components and curricula.

(2) Candidate Content, Pedagogical, and Professional Knowledge, Skills, and Dispositions

   i. *Content Standards* Programs ensure that prospective special educators have mastered the CEC Special Education Content Standards for their respective roles.

   ii. *Liberal Education* Programs ensure that prospective special educators have a solid grounding in the liberal curricula ensuring proficiency in reading, written and oral communications, calculating, problem solving, and thinking.

iii. *General Curriculum*

   (a) Programs ensure that prospective special educators possess a solid base of understanding of the general content area curricula (i.e., math, reading, English/ language arts, science, social studies, and the arts), sufficient to collaborate with general educators in:

     Teaching or collaborative teaching academic subject matter content of the general curriculum to individuals with exceptional learning needs across a wide range of performance levels

     Designing appropriate learning and performance accommodations and modifications for individuals with exceptional learning needs in academic subject matter content of the general curriculum

   (b) Programs preparing special educators for secondary level practice and licensure in which the teachers may assume sole responsibility for teaching academic subject matter classes, ensure that the prospective special educators have a subject matter content knowledge base sufficient to assure that individuals with exceptional learning needs can meet state curriculum standards.

(3) **Assessment System and Program Evaluation**

Programs have an assessment system to collect and analyze data on the applicant qualifications, candidates and graduate performance, and program operations sufficient to evaluate and improve the program.

(4) **Field Experiences and Clinical Practice**

Programs with their school partners have designed, implemented, and evaluated field experiences and clinical practica sufficient for prospective special educators to develop and apply knowledge, skills, and dispositions essential to the roles for which they are being prepared.

(5) **Diversity**

Programs with their school partners have designed, implemented, and evaluated curriculum and experiences sufficient for prospective special educators to develop and apply their knowledge, skills, and dispositions necessary to help all individuals with exceptional learning needs learn. The curricula and experiences include working with diverse faculty, candidates, and P–12 individuals with exceptional learning needs.

(6) **Faculty Qualification, Performance, and Development**

The program faculty is qualified and model best professional practice in their scholarship, service, and teaching.

(7) **Program Governance and Resources**

The program has appropriate leadership, authority, budget, facilities, and resources to address professional, institutional, and state standards.

CEC policy approved October 2004.

Association of Teacher Educators Standards for Teacher Educators

To help all teacher candidates and other school personnel impact student learning, accomplished teacher educators demonstrate the following nine standards:

Accomplished Teacher Educators . . .

STANDARD 1   TEACHING

Model teaching that demonstrates content and professional knowledge, skills, and dispositions reflecting research, proficiency with technology and assessment, and accepted best practices in teacher education.

In order for teacher educators to impact the profession, they must successfully model appropriate behaviors in order for those behaviors to be observed, adjusted, replicated, internalized, and applied appropriately to learners of all levels and styles. "Modeling means exhibiting behavior that is observed and imitated by others" (Kauchak & Eggen, 2005, p. 396). Effective modeling of desired practices is at the heart of successful teacher education programs at pre-service and in-service levels. Teachers are powerful and meaningful role models for students at all levels, and the way they act influences both learning and motivation (Bandura, 1989). Modeling of behavior relates to teaching, service, and scholarly productivity. Teacher educators must use research-based, proven best practices in order for those behaviors to be appropriately applied.

Reprinted with permission from Association of Teacher Educators. (2007). *Standards for teacher educators*. Available at *www.ate1.org/pubs/uploads/tchredstds0308.pdf*.

Kauchak, D., & Eggen, P. (2005). *Introduction to teaching: Becoming a professional.* Upper Saddle River, NJ: Pearson Education.

Bandura, A. (1989). Social cognitive theory. In R. Vasta (Ed.), *Annals of child development* (Vol. 6, pp. 1–60). Greenwich, CT: JAI Press.

Indicators

- Model effective instruction to meet the needs of diverse learners
- Demonstrate and promote critical thinking and problem solving among teacher educators, teachers, and/or prospective teachers
- Revise courses to incorporate current research and/or best practices
- Model reflective practice to foster student reflection
- Demonstrate appropriate subject matter content
- Demonstrate appropriate and accurate professional content in the teaching field
- Demonstrate a variety of instructional and assessment methods including use of technology
- Mentor novice teachers and/or teacher educators
- Facilitate professional development experiences related to effective teaching practices
- Ground practice in current policy and research related to education and teacher education

Artifacts

- Evaluations from supervisors, colleagues, students, or others
- Course syllabi
- Video and/or audiotapes of teaching
- Developed instructional materials (e.g., lessons, units, courses of study, presentations)
- Testimonials
- Teaching awards and/or other forms of recognition
- Logs or other documentation of classroom activities
- Journals of reflective practice
- Philosophical statement that reflects underlying knowledge and values of teacher education
- Relevant credentials (e.g., certificates, licenses)
- Evidence of technology-based teaching and learning

STANDARD 2   CULTURAL COMPETENCE

Apply cultural competence and promote social justice in teacher education.

One of the charges to teacher education is to prepare teachers to connect and communicate with diverse learners (Darling-Hammond & Bransford, 2005). To develop capacity among culturally, socially, and linguistically diverse students, teachers first need to know their own cultures. They also need to hold high expectations for all students, understand developmental levels and what is common and unique among different groups, reach out to families and communities to learn about their cultures, select curriculum materials that are inclusive, use a range of assessment methods, and be proficient in a variety of pedagogical methods that facilitate the acquisition of content knowledge for all learners. Establishing a closer fit between pedagogy and culturally different learning styles positively impacts students both socially and academically (Gay, 2002). Culturally relevant pedagogy "not only addresses student achievement but also helps students to accept and affirm their cultural identity while developing critical perspectives that challenge inequities that schools (and other institutions) perpetuate" (Ladson-Billings, 1995, p. 469). Teacher educators share the responsibility of helping pre-service and in-service teachers to understand these concepts and to apply them successfully in their classrooms. They do not merely understand the concepts underlying the definitions of cultural competency but clearly demonstrate how those concepts are applied in their own teaching and in that of their students.

Darling-Hammond, L., & Bransford, J. (2005). *Preparing teachers for a changing world: What teachers should learn and be able to do.* San Francisco: Jossey-Bass.

Gay, G. (2005). *A synthesis of scholarship in multicultural education.* Naperville, IL: North Central Regional Educational Laboratory.

Ladson-Billings, G. (1995). Toward a theory of culturally relevant pedagogy. *American Educational Research Journal, 32*(3), 465–491.

Indicators

- Exhibit practices that enhance both an understanding of diversity and instruction that meets the needs of society
- Engage in culturally responsive pedagogy
- Professionally participate in diverse communities
- Model ways to reduce prejudice for pre-service and in-service teachers and/or other educational professionals
- Engage in activities that promote social justice
- Demonstrate connecting instruction to students' families, cultures, and communities
- Model how to identify and design instruction appropriate to students' stages of development, learning styles, linguistic skills, strengths and needs
- Foster a positive regard for individual students and their families regardless of differences such as culture, religion, gender, native language, sexual orientation, and varying abilities
- Demonstrate knowledge of their own culture and aspects common to all cultures and foster such knowledge in others
- Promote inquiry into cultures and differences
- Teach a variety of assessment tools that meet the needs of diverse learners
- Recruit diverse teachers and teacher educators

Artifacts

- Course syllabi
- Instructional materials

- Evidence of involvement in schools and other organizations with diverse populations
- Video and/or audio tapes of teaching
- Course assignments
- Student work samples
- Evidence of involvement in school based projects and/or service learning
- Evidence of providing professional development to others at all levels
- Philosophical statement that reflects underlying that reflects attention to diversity
- Assessment tools appropriate for use with diverse learners

STANDARD 3   SCHOLARSHIP

Engage in inquiry and contribute to scholarship that expands the knowledge base related to teacher education.

The scholarship of an accomplished teacher educator is conceptualized through Boyer's model of scholarship (1997) which includes four foci: discovery, integration, application, and teaching. Accomplished teacher educators continually ask questions to deepen existing knowledge and to create new knowledge in teaching and teacher education. This is achieved through systematic inquiry and the subsequent sharing and/or dissemination of the results. Teacher educators engage in discourse within a community about the quest for new knowledge. This community, for example, can be broadly defined as a community of academics whose discourse takes place within publications or a community of inquirers who dialogue around their "reflection on action" (Schön, 1983). In addition to discourse around new knowledge, teacher educators integrate their learning about practice within the field of teacher education together with their knowledge across disciplines and contexts in order to elucidate connections between their own work and the broader educational landscape. Teacher educators bridge their theoretical and practical knowledge to create new understandings and interpretations in theory and practice of teaching and teacher education. Finally, accomplished teacher educators strive to teach others and to foster learning about teaching and teacher education.

Boyer, E. L. (1997). *Scholarship reconsidered: Priorities of the professoriate.* San Francisco: Jossey-Bass.
Schön, D. A. (1983). *The reflective practitioner: How professionals think in action.* New York: Basic Books.

Indicators

- Investigate theoretical and practical problems in teaching, learning, and/or teacher education
- Pursue new knowledge in relation to teaching, learning, and/or teacher education
- Connect new knowledge to existing contexts and perspectives
- Engage in research and development projects
- Apply research to teaching practice and/or program or curriculum development
- Conduct program evaluation
- Acquire research-based and service-based grants

- Disseminate research findings to the broader teacher education community
- Engage in action research
- Systematically assess learning goals and outcomes

Artifacts

- Publications
- Presentations at meetings of learned societies or specialized professional associations
- Citations by other scholars
- Professional development workshops and/or seminars
- Speaking engagements that focus on issues of teacher education
- Evidence of improved teaching practice
- Evidence of increased student learning
- Research-based program development
- Funded grant proposals
- Research awards or recognitions
- National Board Certification

STANDARD 4   PROFESSIONAL DEVELOPMENT

Inquire systematically into, reflect on, and improve their own practice and demonstrate commitment to continuous professional development.

Accomplished teacher educators help pre-service and in-service teachers with professional development and reflection, and model examples from their personal development, making transparent the goals, information, and changes for improvements in their own teaching. Teacher educators examine their own beliefs and contributions of life experiences. There is a vital link established between belief and action (Vygotsky, 1978). Reflective practice of teachers can occur in several forms and at different times during and after an event, and should be proactive in nature to guide any future action (Farrell, 2004). Reflection can affect professional growth and bring individuals to greater self-actualization (Pedro, 2006) through collaboration with others to apply knowledge and experiences into practice (Schön, 1996). Experience is key to developing thinking (Dewey, 1916) and helping educators to form knowledge, collect data, reflect on that data, and make changes to their practices.

Dewey, J. (1916). *Democracy and education.* New York: Macmillan.

Farrell, T. S. C. (2004). *Reflective practice in action: 80 reflection breaks for busy teachers.* Thousand Oaks, CA: Corwin Press.

Pedro, J. (2006). Taking reflection into the real world of teaching. *Kappa Delta Pi Record, 42*(3), 129–133.

Schön, D. A. (1996). *Educating the reflective practitioner: Toward a new design for teaching and learning in the professions.* San Francisco: Jossey-Bass.

Vygotsky, L. (1978). *Mind in society: The development of higher psychological processes.* Cambridge, MA: Harvard University Press.

Indicators

- Systematically reflect on own practice and learning
- Engage in purposeful professional development focused on professional learning goals
- Develop and maintain a philosophy of teaching and learning that is continuously reviewed based on a deepening understanding of research and practice
- Participate in and reflect on learning activities in professional associations and learned societies
- Apply life experiences to teaching and learning

Artifacts

- Statement of philosophy of teaching and learning
- Evidence of professional development goals and activities
- Self-assessment
- Evidence of documented professional growth
- Evidence of participation in professional development experiences
- Letter of support
- Reflective journals

STANDARD 5   PROGRAM DEVELOPMENT

Provide leadership in developing, implementing, and evaluating teacher education programs that are rigorous, relevant, and grounded in theory, research, and best practice.

The foundation of the professional work of teacher educators lies in development and maintenance of quality programs that prepare beginning teachers and provide for teachers' on-going professional development during and after induction into the profession. Accomplished teacher educators are regular contributors to and often leaders in the development, refinement, and revision of programs and portions of programs focused on initial teacher preparation and on-going teacher professional development. The development of quality teacher education programs that serve teachers at all stages in their career is at the heart of the ATE's mission (Selke & Alouf, 2004). It is through these programs that teachers learn and further develop the content and pedagogical knowledge, understandings, and skills they need. Research and program evaluation must be gathered and applied to make data-driven decisions to benefit individual programs and the overall profession.

Selke, M., & Alouf, J. (2004). *Position framework: ATE.* Retrieved June 8, 2006, from *www.ate1.org/pubs/ATE_Position_Frame.cfm.*

Indicators

- Design, develop, or modify teacher education programs based on theory, research, and best practice
- Provide leadership in obtaining approval or accreditation for new or modified teacher education programs

- Lead or actively contribute to the ongoing assessment of teacher education courses or programs
- Provide leadership that focuses on establishing standards for teacher education programs or on developing, approving, and accrediting teacher education programs at the local, state, national, or international level
- Contribute to research that focuses on effective teacher education programs

Artifacts

- Course or program proposal
- Revision to course or program
- New materials developed to meet course or program requirements
- Evidence of participation in program development, revision, or evaluation
- Document of leadership in program accreditation process (state or national)
- Program recognition or award
- Evidence of participation in research on or evaluation study of a teacher education program
- Publications, handouts, or other documentation of conference presentations on program development

STANDARD 6   COLLABORATION

Collaborate regularly and in significant ways with relevant stakeholders to improve teaching, research, and student learning.

Accomplished teacher educators adopt a collaborative approach to teacher education that involves a variety of stakeholders (e.g., universities, schools, families, communities, foundations, businesses, and museums) in teaching and learning. Collaboration to design and implement teacher education promotes the collective practice that increases efficacy and knowledge of teacher education. This facilitates a sense of trust and draws on the expertise of different stakeholders within the collaboration (Fullan & Hargreaves, 1991). Professional relationships foster a community of collaboration in which teacher educators make explicit their work and increase self-learning and knowledge. Collaboration is often formalized in partnerships that join individuals and institutions to work together on a long term basis. In the education of teachers, collaboration and partnerships exist in pre-service teacher education as well as the continuing education of induction and in-service teachers.

Fullan M., & Hargreaves, A. (Eds.). (1992). *Teacher development and educational change.* New York: Falmer Press.

Indicators

- Engage in cross-institutional and cross-college partnerships
- Support teacher education in the P–12 school environment
- Participate in joint decision making about teacher education

- Foster cross-disciplinary endeavors
- Engage in reciprocal relationships in teacher education
- Initiate collaborative projects that contribute to improved teacher education
- Acquire financial support for teacher education innovation to support collaboration

Artifacts

- Evidence of collaborative activities (e.g., minutes and agenda of meetings)
- Testimonials
- Records of awards, recognition, and financial support for research resulting from collaboration
- Course syllabi that demonstrate collaboration
- Joint publications resulting from collaboration

STANDARD 7   PUBLIC ADVOCACY

Serve as informed, constructive advocates for high quality education for all students.

Teacher educators advocate both within and outside of the profession for high quality education for all students at all levels. Influencing decision makers and promoting changes to laws and other government policies to advance the mission of a high quality education for all is paramount to the profession. Such advocacy requires being informed with respect to social and political perceptions, policies, challenges, and systems that affect education (Cochran-Smith, 2004). Acquiring research-based background information should be the basis for advocacy at all levels. As Laitsch et al. (2002) have pointed out, research has long been supported as the basis for decision-making in educational forums. Accomplished teacher educators engage in active advocacy for quality education, which clearly articulates appropriate responses addressing educational concerns and visions for contemporary and future stakeholders. This advocacy promotes quality education for all students in local, state, regional, national, and international venues. Through reflection and revision of information and efforts, teacher educators actively assess their personal impact on educational reform.

Cochran-Smith, M. (2004). Taking stock in 2004: Teacher education in dangerous times. *Journal of Teacher Education, 55*(1), 3–7.

Laitsch, D., Heilman, E., & Shaker, P. (2002). Teacher Education, pro-market policy and advocacy research. *Teaching Education, 13*(3), 251–271.

Indicators

- Promote quality education for all learners through community forums, activities with other professionals, and work with local policy makers
- Inform and educate those involved in making governmental policies and regulations at local, state, and/or national levels to support and improve teaching and learning
- Actively address policy issues which affect the education profession

Artifacts

- Evidence of advocacy for high quality teaching and learning in local, state, national, and/or international settings
- Evidence of contributions to educational policy or regulations at local, state, national, and/or international levels
- Papers, presentations, and/or media events designed to enhance the public's understanding of teaching and learning
- Evidence of service to school accreditation committees
- Scholarship and/or grant activity promoting education

STANDARD 8   TEACHER EDUCATION PROFESSION

Contribute to improving the teacher education profession.

Through a visionary and collaborative approach, accomplished teacher educators accept responsibility for improving their profession. They make a difference by attending to the complexities and vulnerabilities of the profession (Covey, 1989, p. 299). Teacher educators share a responsibility for active service as members of local, state, and national professional organizations. These affiliations offer a venue for professional identification and support to improve the teacher education profession. Collective membership in professional organizations contributes to the strength of teacher education Teacher educators are vested with authority in teacher education and their technical expertise qualifies the profession for determination of the public good (Bellah, 1985, p. 195)

Bellah, R. N., Madsen, R., Sullivan, W. M., Swidler, A., & Tipton, S. M. (1985). *Habits of the heart: Individualism and commitment in American life*. New York: Harper & Row.
Covey, S. R. (1989). *The seven habits of highly effective people: Powerful lessons for personal change*. New York: Simon & Schuster.

Indicators

- Actively participate in professional organizations at the local, state, national, or international level
- Edit/review manuscripts for publication or presentation for teacher education organizations
- Review resources designed to advance the profession
- Develop textbook or multimedia resource for use in teacher education
- Recruit promising pre-service teachers
- Recruit future teacher educators
- Mentor colleagues toward professional excellence
- Design and/or implement pre-service and induction programs for teachers
- Support student organizations to advance teacher education
- Advocate for high quality teacher education standards

Artifacts

- Evidence of active participation in professional organizations
- Conference programs and proceedings
- Books/monographs/periodicals edited or reviewed
- Textbook/multimedia reviews
- Textbooks and multimedia resources developed
- Testimonials
- Evidence of support of student organizations
- Grant proposals
- Reports and evaluations of projects/advancement programs
- Records of awards/recognition for excellence in teacher education

STANDARD 9   VISION

Contribute to creating visions for teaching, learning, and teacher education that take into account such issues as technology, systemic thinking, and world views.

Accomplished teacher educators develop essential insights into the vast changes occurring today. They embrace them, visualize their potential for education, and interpret them to pre-service and in-service teachers in order to facilitate understanding and integration into professional practice. Technology and miniaturization affect all aspects of society. The debate over the relative importance of content for future generations needs to be focused by knowledgeable teacher educators who understand history, teaching, research, and technology. A critical factor is the increasing impact of globalization on education (Friedman, 2005). Education has traditionally followed rather than led changes in society. Accomplished teacher educators embrace their role as change agents, understand the impact teacher education has on classroom practices, and are early adopters of new configurations of learning (Rogers, 2003). Accomplished teacher educators are firmly in the forefront of educational change.

Friedman, T. L. (2005). *The world is flat*. New York: Farrar, Straus, & Giroux.
Rogers, E. M. (2003). *Diffusion of innovations* (5th ed.). New York: Free Press.

Indicators

- Actively participate in learning communities that focus on educational change
- Demonstrate innovation in the field of teacher education
- Demonstrate qualities of an early adopter of technology and new configurations of learning
- Actively pursue new knowledge of global issues
- Support innovation adoption with research
- Relate new knowledge about global issues to own practice and K–12 classroom teaching

Artifacts

- Grant writing activity
- Evidence of participation in learning communities
- Reflection journals
- Course syllabi
- Course assignments
- Student work samples
- Evidence of self-directed learning in innovative methodologies
- Evidence of using new and evolving technologies or content in teaching and learning

Council for Exceptional Children Code of Ethics

Professional special educators are guided by the CEC professional ethical principles and practice standards in ways that respect the diverse characteristics and needs of individuals with exceptionalities and their families. They are committed to upholding and advancing the following principles:

A. Maintaining challenging expectations for individuals with exceptionalities to develop the highest possible learning outcomes and quality of life potential in ways that respect their dignity, culture, language, and background.

B. Maintaining a high level of professional competence and integrity and exercising professional judgment to benefit individuals with exceptionalities and their families.

C. Promoting meaningful and inclusive participation of individuals with exceptionalities in their schools and communities.

D. Practicing collegially with others who are providing services to individuals with exceptionalities.

E. Developing relationships with families based on mutual respect and actively involving families and individuals with exceptionalities in educational decision making.

F. Using evidence, instructional data, research and professional knowledge to inform practice.

Reprinted with permission from Council for Exceptional Children. (2010). *Special education professional ethical principles.* Available at *www.cec.sped.org/Content/NavigationMenu/Profession-alDevelopment/ProfessionalStandards/EthicsPracticeStandards/Ethical_Principles_2010.pdf.*

G. Protecting and supporting the physical and psychological safety of individuals with exceptionalities.

H. Neither engaging in nor tolerating any practice that harms individuals with exceptionalities.

I. Practicing within the professional ethics, standards, and policies of CEC; upholding laws, regulations, and policies that influence professional practice; and advocating improvements in laws, regulations, and policies.

J. Advocating for professional conditions and resources that will improve learning outcomes of individuals with exceptionalities.

K. Engaging in the improvement of the profession through active participation in professional organizations.

L. Participating in the growth and dissemination of professional knowledge and skills.

References

Americans with Disabilities Act of 1990, as Amended Public Law No. 110-325. (2009). Retrieved September 29, 2010, from *www.ada.gov/pubs/ada.htm*.

Angelo, T. A., & Cross, K. P. (1993). *Classroom assessment techniques: A handbook for college teachers* (2nd ed.). San Francisco: Jossey-Bass.

Association of Teacher Educators (ATE). (2007). *Standards for teacher educators*. Retrieved August 28, 2009, from *www. ate1. org/pubs/uploads/tchredstds0308. pdf*.

Bateman, B. D., & Herr, C. M. (2006). *Writing measureable IEP goals and objectives* (2nd ed.). Verona, WI: Attainment.

Beck, C., & Kosnick, C. (2006). *Innovations in teacher education: A social constructivist approach.* Albany, NY: SUNY Press.

Begley, S. (2007). *Train your mind, change your brain: How a new science reveals our extraordinary potential to transform ourselves.* New York: Random House.

Bergeron, B. S., Larson, B., Prest, A., Dumas-Hopper, L. A., & Wenhart, J. C. (2005). Innovation in teacher preparation: Creating alternative routes to teacher quality. In J. R. Dangel & E. M. Guyton (Eds.), *Research on alternative and non-traditional education: Teacher education yearbook XIII* (pp. 59–72). Lanham, MD: Association of Teacher Educators.

Berry, B., Norton, J., & Byrd, A. (2007). Lessons from networking. *Educational Leadership, 65*(1), 48–52.

Billingsley, B. (2001). *Beginning special educators: Characteristics, qualifications, and experiences. SPeNSE summary sheet.* Rockville, MD: Westat. Retrieved July 28, 2011, from *www.eric.ed.gov* (ERIC No. ED467269).

Billingsley, B. S. (2004). Special education teachers' retention and attrition: A critical analysis of the research literature. *The Journal of Special Education, 38,* 39–55.

Billingsley, B. S. (2005). *Cultivating and keeping committed special education teachers: What principals and district leaders can do.* Thousand Oaks, CA: Corwin Press.

147

Blanton, L., Sindelar, P. T., Correa, V., Hardman, M., McDonnell, J., & Kuhel, K. (2003). *Conceptions of beginning teacher quality: Models of conducting research* (COPSSE Document Number RS-6E). Gainesville: University of Florida, Center on Personnel Studies in Special Education.

Boe, E. E. (2006). Long-term trends in the national demand, supply, and shortage of special education teachers. *The Journal of Special Education, 40,* 138–150.

Boyd, D., Lankford, H., Loeb, S., & Wyckoff, J. (2005). The draw of home: How teachers' preferences for proximity disadvantage urban schools. *Journal of Policy Analysis and Management, 24,* 113–132.

Boyer, L., & Mainzer, R. W. (2003). Who's teaching students with disabilities?: A profile of characteristics, licensure status, and feelings of preparedness. *Teaching Exceptional Children, 35,* 8–11.

Bradley, J. F., & Monda-Amaya, L. E. (2005). Conflict resolution: Preparing preservice special educators to work in collaborative settings. *Teacher Education and Special Education, 28,* 171–184.

Brownell, M. T., Bishop, A. G., & Sindelar, P. T. (2004, October). *Beginning teacher quality in special education: Implications for initial preparation.* Presentation at the Annual Meeting of the Council for Learning Disabilities, Las Vegas, NV.

Brownell, M. T., Ross, D. D., Colón, E. P., & McCallum, C. L. (2003). *Critical features of special education teacher preparation: A comparison with exemplary practices in general teacher education* (COPSSE Document Number RS-4E). Gainesville: University of Florida, Center on Personnel Studies in Special Education.

Brownell, M. T., Ross, D. D., Colón, E. P., & McCallum, C. L. (2005). Critical features of special education teacher preparation: A comparison with general teacher education. *The Journal of Special Education, 38,* 242–252.

Brownell, M. T., Sindelar, P. T., Kiely, M. T., & Danielson, L. C. (2010). Special education teacher quality and preparation: Exposing foundations, constructing a new model. *Exceptional Children, 76,* 357–377.

Burns, M. K., & Haight, S. L. (2005). Psychometric properties and instructional utility of assessing special education teacher candidate knowledge with portfolios. *Teacher Education and Special Education, 28,* 185–194.

Cochran-Smith, M. (2003). Learning and unlearning: The education of teacher educators. *Teaching and Teacher Education, 19,* 5–28.

Cochran-Smith, M., & Zeichner, K. M. (Eds.). (2005). *Studying teacher education: The report of the AERA panel on research and teacher education.* Mahwah, NJ: Erlbaum.

Connelly, V. J., & Rosenberg, M. S. (2003). *Developing teaching as a profession: Comparison with careers that have achieved full professional standing* (COPSSE Document Number RS-9E). Gainesville: University of Florida, Center on Personnel Studies in Special Education.

Cook, L. H., & Boe, E. H. (2007). National trends in the sources of supply of teachers in special and general education. *Teacher Education and Special Education, 30,* 217–232.

Council for Exceptional Children (CEC). (2003). *What every special educator must know: The international standards for the preparation and certification of special education teachers* (5th ed.). Arlington, VA: Author.

Council for Exceptional Children (CEC). (2009). *What every special educator must know: Ethics, standards, and guidelines* (6th ed., rev.). Arlington, VA: Author.

Cruickshank, D. R. (1996). *Preparing America's teachers*. Bloomington, IN: Phi Delta Kappa Educational Foundation.

Darling-Hammond, L. (2006). *Powerful teacher education: Lessons from exemplary programs*. San Francisco: Jossey-Bass.

Darling-Hammond, L., & Baratz-Snowden, J. (Eds.). (2005). *A good teacher in every classroom: Preparing the highly qualified teachers our children deserve*. San Francisco: Jossey-Bass.

Deshler, D. D., & Shumaker, J. B. (2006). *Teaching adolescents with disabilities: Accessing the general education curriculum* Thousand Oaks, CA: Corwin Press.

Dickar, M. (2005). When they are good . . . : A comparison of career changers and recent college graduates in an alternative certification program. In J. R. Dangel & E. M. Guyton (Eds.), *Research on alternative and non-traditional education: Teacher education yearbook XIII* (pp. 91–104). Lanham, MD: Association of Teacher Educators.

Dinkelman, T., Margolis, J., & Sikkenga, K. (2006). From teacher to teacher educator: Experiences, expectations, and expatriation. *Studying Teacher Education, 2,* 5–23.

Duffy, M. L., & Forgan, J. (2005). *Mentoring new special education teachers: A guide for mentors and program developers*. Thousand Oaks, CA: Corwin Press.

Educational Testing Service (ETS). (n.d.). *www.ets.org*.

Evans, S., Andrews, L., Miller, N., & Smith, S. (2003). An alternative model for preparing special education teacher educators. *Teacher Education and Special Education, 26,* 150–153.

Feng, L., Figlio, D. N., & Sass, T. R. (2010). *School accountability and teacher mobility* (Working Paper No. 47). National Center for Analysis of Longitudinal Data in Education Research. (ERIC No. ED510550)

Fiedler, C., & Van Haren, B. (2009). A comparison of special education administrators' and teachers' knowledge and application of ethics and professional standards. *The Journal of Special Education, 43,* 160–173.

Friend, M. (2007). The co-teaching partnership. *Educational Leadership, 64,* 48–52.

Friend, M., & Cook, L. (2010). *Interactions: Collaboration skills for school professionals* (6th ed.). Boston: Allyn & Bacon.

Gavins, M. V. (2007). *IEP development as a function of pedagogical experience in special education teachers*. Unpublished doctoral dissertation, University of Maryland–College Park.

Gehrke, R., & Murri, N. (2006). Beginning special educators' intent to stay in special education: Why they like it here. *Teacher Education and Special Education, 29,* 179–190.

Greer, D., & Meyen, E. (2009). Special education teacher education: A perspective on content knowledge. *Learning Disabilities Research and Practice, 24,* 196–203.

Griffin, C. C., & Pugach, M. C. (2007). Framing the progress of collaborative teacher education. *Focus on Exceptional Children, 39*(6), 1–12.

Grossman, P. (2005). Research on pedagogical approaches in teacher education. In M. Cochran-Smith & K. M. Zeichner (Eds.), *Studying teacher education: The report of the AERA panel on research and teacher education* (pp. 425–476). Mahwah, NJ: Erlbaum.

Guskey, T. R. (2000). *Evaluating professional development*. Thousand Oaks, CA: Corwin Press.

Hardman, M. L., & West, J. (2003). Increasing the number of special education faculty:

Policy implications and future directions. *Teacher Education and Special Education, 26,* 206–214.

Individuals with Disabilities Education Improvement Act (IDEIA) of 2004, Public Law No. 108-446. (2004). Retrieved July 5, 2010, from *www.gpo.gov/fdsys/pkg/PLAW-108publ446/pdf/PLAW-108publ446.pdf.*

The IRIS Center for Training Enhancements. (n. d.). *SRSD: Using learning strategies: Instruction to enhance student learning.* Retrieved July 27, 2011, from *iris.peabody.vanderbilt.edu/srs/chalcycle.htm.*

Israel, M. (2009). *Preparation of special education teacher educators: An investigation of emerging signature pedagogies.* Unpublished doctoral dissertation, University of Kansas, Lawrence.

Johnson, L. J., & Bauer, A. M. (Eds.). (2003). Study of special education leadership personnel [Special issue]. *Teacher Education and Special Education, 26*(3).

Kewal Ramani, A., Gilbertson, L., Fox, M., & Provasnik, S. (2007). *Status and Trends in the Education of Racial and Ethnic Minorities* (NCES 2007-039). Washington, DC: U.S. Department of Education, National Center for Education Statistics, Institute of Education Sciences.

Kirkwood, A., & Price, L. (2005). Learners and learning in the twenty-first century: What do we know about students' attitudes towards and experiences of information and communication technologies that will help us design courses? *Studies in Higher Education, 30,* 257–274.

Kleinhammer-Tramill, J., Tramill, J., & Brace, H. (2010). Contexts, funding history, and implications for evaluating the office of special education program's investment in personnel preparation. *The Journal of Special Education, 43,* 195–205.

Knapczyk, D. R., Hew, K. F., Frey, T. J., & Wall-Marencik, W. (2005). Evaluation of online mentoring of practicum for limited licensed teachers. *Teacher Education and Special Education, 28,* 207–220.

Korir Bore, J. C. (2008). Perceptions of graduate students on the use of web-based instruction in special education personnel preparation. *Teacher Education and Special Education, 31,* 1–11.

Kossar, K. (2003). Graduate practicum—special education: Assessment through portfolio development. *Teacher Education and Special Education, 26,* 145–149.

Lampert, M. (2001). *Teaching problems and the problems of teaching.* New Haven, CT: Yale University Press.

Lava, V. F., Recchia, S. L., & Giovacco-Johnson, T. (2004). Early childhood special educators reflect on their preparation and practice. *Teacher Education and Special Education, 27,* 190–201.

Leko, M. M. (2008). *Understanding the various influences on special education preservice teachers' appropriation of conceptual and practical tools for teaching reading.* Unpublished doctoral dissertation, University of Florida, Gainesville.

Lenz, B. K., Deshler, D. D., & Kissam, B. R. (2004). *Teaching content to all: Evidence-based inclusive practices in middle and secondary schools.* Boston: Pearson/Allyn & Bacon.

Loughran, J., & Berry, A. (2005). Modeling by teacher educators. *Teaching and Teacher Education, 21,* 193–203.

Mabe, A. (2007, September). *Keynote address.* Presented at the 25th Annual NC Teacher Forum, Raleigh, NC.

Mamlin, N. L. (1995). *A restructuring initiative focusing on special education: One school's interpretations of inclusion and change.* Unpublished doctoral dissertation, University of Maryland–College Park.

Mamlin, N. (1999). Despite best intentions: When inclusion fails. *The Journal of Special Education, 33*, 36–49.

Mamlin, N. (2009, April). *Are textbooks changing with the times?: An evaluation of common texts.* Poster presented at the Annual Meeting of the Council for Exceptional Children, Seattle.

Marshall, S. P. (2005). A decidedly different mind. *Shift: At the Frontiers of Consciousness, 8*, 10 -15.

Martinez, K. (2008). Academic induction for teacher educators. *Asia-Pacific Journal of Teacher Education, 36*, 35–51.

Mastropieri, M. A. (2001). Is the glass half full or half empty? Challenges encountered by first-year special education teachers. *The Journal of Special Education, 35*, 66–74.

McLaughlin, M. J., & Nolet, V. (2004). *What every principal needs to know about special education.* Thousand Oaks, CA: Corwin Press.

Meyen, E. (2007, November). *The TED legacy study: Leadership perspectives on the changing landscape in teacher education.* Keynote address presented at the Annual Meeting of the Teacher Education Division of the Council for Exceptional Children, Milwaukee, WI.

Miller, M. D., Brownell, M. T., & Smith, S. (1999). Factors that predict teachers staying in, leaving, or transferring from the special education classroom. *Exceptional Children, 65*, 201–218.

Monaco, M., & Martin, M. (2007). The millennial student: A new generation of learners. *Athletic Training Education Journal, 2*, 42–46.

Murdock, S. H., & Hoque, M. N. (1999). Demographic factors affecting higher education in the United States in the twenty-first century. *New Directions for Higher Education, 108*, 5–13.

National Commission on Teaching and America's Future. (2003). *No dream denied: A pledge to America's children.* New York: Author.

Nougaret, A., Scruggs, T., & Mastropieri, M. (2005). Does teacher education produce better special education teachers? *Exceptional Children, 71*, 217–229.

Oblinger, D. G., & Oblinger, J. L. (2005). *Educating the net generation.* Available from *www.educause.edu/educatingthenetgen*.

Pion, G. M., Smith, D. D., & Tyler, N. C. (2003). Career choices of recent doctorates in special education: Their implications for addressing faculty shortages. *Teacher Education and Special Education, 26*, 182–193.

Provenzo, E. F., & Blanton, W. E. (2006). *Observing in schools: A guide for students in teacher education.* Boston: Pearson Education.

Pugach, M. (2005). Research on preparing teachers to work with students with disabilities. In M. Cochran-Smith & K. M. Zeichner (Eds.), *Studying teacher education: The report of the AERA panel on research and teacher education* (pp. 549–590). Mahwah, NJ: Erlbaum.

Rehabilitation Act. (1973). (Public Law No. 93-112). Retrieved September 29, 2010, from *www.dotcr.ost.dot.gov/documents/ycr/REHABACT.HTM*.

Ritter, J. K. (2007). Forging a pedagogy of education: The challenges of moving from classroom teacher to teacher educator. *Studying Teacher Education, 3*, 5–22.

Rosenberg, M., & Sindelar, P. (2005). The proliferation of alternative routes to certification in special education: A critical review of the literature. *The Journal of Special Education, 39*, 117–127.

Rosenberg, M. S., O'Shea, L., & O'Shea, D. J. (2006). *Student teacher to master teacher* (4th ed.). New York: Merrill/Prentice Hall.

Santangelo, T., Harris, K., & Graham, S. (2007). Self-regulated strategy development: A validated model to support students who struggle with writing. *Learning Disabilities: A Contemporary Journal, 5*, 1–20.

Sindelar, P. T., Brownell, M. T., & Billingsley, M. T. (2010). Special education teacher education research: Current status and future directions. *Teacher Education and Special Education, 33*, 8–24.

Sindelar, P. T., & Rosenberg, M. S. (2000). Serving too many masters: The proliferation of ill-conceived and contradictory policies and practices in teacher education. *Journal of Teacher Education, 51*, 188–193.

Smith, D. D., Pion, G. M., Tyler, N. C., & Gilmore, R. (2003). Doctoral programs in special education: The nation's supplier. *Teacher Education and Special Education, 26*, 172–181.

Spooner, M. (2005). Overview and framework: Successes and challenges for alternative routes to certification. In J. R. Dangel & E. M. Guyton (Eds.), *Research on alternative and non-traditional education: Teacher education yearbook XIII* (pp. 3–9). Lanham, MD: Association of Teacher Educators.

Sun, L., Bender, W., & Fore, C. (2003). Web-based certification courses: The future of teacher preparation in special education? *Teacher Education and Special Education, 26*, 87–97.

Swanson, H. L., & Hoskyn, M. (1998). Experimental intervention research on students with learning disabilities: A meta-analysis of treatment outcomes. *Review of Educational Research, 68*, 277–321.

Swanson, H. L., & Sachse-Lee, C. (2000). A meta-analysis of single-subject-design intervention research for students with LD. *Journal of Learning Disabilities, 33*, 114–136.

Thiagarajan, S., Semmel, D. S., & Semmel, M. I. (1974). *Instructional development for training teachers of exceptional children: A sourcebook*. Reston, VA: Council for Exceptional Children.

Trent, S., Kea, C., & Oh, K. (2008). Preparing preservice educators for cultural diversity: How far have we come? *Exceptional Children, 74*, 328–350.

U.S. Department of Education. (2007). *Individuals with Disabilities Education Act (IDEA) data*. Retrieved June 23, 2010, from *www.ideadata.org*.

U.S. Department of Education, National Center for Education Statistics. (2010). *Digest of Education Statistics, 2009* (NCES 2010-013), *Chapter 2*. Retrieved October 8, 2010, from *nces.ed.gov/fastfacts/display.asp?id=59*.

Werts, M. G., Mamlin, N., & Pogoloff, S. M. (2002). Knowing what to expect: Introducing preservice teachers to IEP meetings. *Teacher Education and Special Education, 25*, 413–418.

Westat. (2000). *A high-quality teacher for every classroom*. SPeNSE Summary Sheet. Retrieved July 27, 2011, from *www.eric.ed.gov* (ERIC No. ED467-268).

Whitaker, S. D. (2001). Supporting beginning special education teachers. *Focus on Exceptional Children, 34*(4), 1–18.

Zeichner, K. M., & Conklin, H. G. (2005). Teacher education programs. In M. Cochran-Smith & K. M. Zeichner (Eds.), *Studying teacher education: The report of the AERA panel on research and teacher education* (pp. 645–735). Mahwah, NJ: Erlbaum.

Zeichner, K., Melnick, S., & Gomez, M. L. (Eds.). (1996). *Currents of reform in preservice teacher education*. New York: Teachers College Press.

Zirkel, P. A., & Gischlar, K. L. (2008). Due process hearings under the IDEIA: A longitudinal frequency analysis. *Journal of Special Education Leadership, 21,* 22–31.

Index

An *f* following a page number indicates a figure; a *t* following a page number indicates a table.